6/08

The Up and Down Life

The Up and Down Life

The Truth about Bipolar Disorder— the Good, the Bad, and the Funny

PAUL E. JONES

with ANDREA THOMPSON

A Perigee Book

A Lynn Sonberg Book

A PERIGEE BOOK
Published by the Penguin Group
Penguin Group (USA) Inc.
375 Hudson Street, New York, New York 10014, USA
Penguin Group (Canada), 90 Eglinton Avenue East, Suite 700, Toronto, Ontario M4P 2Y3, Canada
(a division of Pearson Penguin Canada Inc.)
Penguin Books Ltd., 80 Strand, London WC2R 0RL, England
Penguin Group Ireland, 25 St. Stephen's Green, Dublin 2, Ireland (a division of Penguin Books Ltd.)
Penguin Group (Australia), 250 Camberwell Road, Camberwell, Victoria 3124, Australia
(a division of Pearson Australia Group Pty. Ltd.)
Penguin Books India Pvt. Ltd., 11 Community Centre, Panchsheel Park, New Delhi—110 017, India
Penguin Group (NZ), 67 Apollo Drive, Rosedale, North Shore 0632, New Zealand
(a division of Pearson New Zealand Ltd.)
Penguin Books (South Africa) (Pty.) Ltd., 24 Sturdee Avenue, Rosebank, Johannesburg 2196, South Africa

Penguin Books Ltd., Registered Offices: 80 Strand, London WC2R 0RL, England

While the author has made every effort to provide accurate telephone numbers and Internet addresses at the time of publication, neither the publisher nor the author assumes any responsibility for errors, or for changes that occur after publication. Further, the publisher does not have any control over and does not assume any responsibility for author or third-party websites or their content.

Copyright © 2008 by ZassCo, Inc., and Lynn Sonberg Book Associates
Text design by Kristin del Rosario

First edition: May 2008

Library of Congress Cataloging-in-Publication Data

Jones, Paul E.
    The up and down life : the truth about bipolar disorder—the good, the bad, and the funny / Paul E. Jones with Andrea Thompson.
        p.   cm.
    "A Lynn Sonberg book."
    ISBN 978-0-399-53422-5
    1. Manic-depressive illness—Popular works.   I. Thompson, Andrea.   II. Title.
    RC516.J66 2008
    616.89'5—dc22   2007043103

PRINTED IN THE UNITED STATES OF AMERICA

10   9   8   7   6   5   4   3   2   1

PUBLISHER'S NOTE: Neither the publisher nor the author is engaged in rendering professional advice or services to the individual reader. The ideas, procedures, and suggestions contained in this book are not intended as a substitute for consulting with your physician. All matters regarding your health require medical supervision. Neither the author nor the publisher shall be liable or responsible for any loss or damage allegedly arising from any information or suggestion in this book.

Most Perigee books are available at special quantity discounts for bulk purchases for sales promotions, premiums, fund-raising, or educational use. Special books, or book excerpts, can also be created to fit specific needs. For details, write: Special Markets, Penguin Group (USA) Inc., 375 Hudson Street, New York, New York 10014.

CONTENTS

FOREWORD

Bipolar disorder is a real and devastating illness, with the potential to disrupt and damage the lives of those who suffer from it and of their loved ones. The good news is that it can be successfully controlled in most cases through accurate diagnosis, medication, and lifestyle changes. Help is out there.

But bipolar disorder is also a tricky, puzzling illness, one that cannot be diagnosed through the physician's usual arsenal of blood tests, MRIs, and similar procedures. Its symptoms include fluctuations in mood and emotions, and erratic behaviors. Its characteristics are such that the individual is likely to think the troublesome aspects of his life are, well, "just life," or just his "personality," or the result of a lack of willpower. And so he doesn't seek treatment or an explanation for what's wrong with him. Or he realizes he should get medical advice, but doesn't know where to turn or how to start.

In *The Up and Down Life*, Paul Jones demonstrates clearly—and in his uniquely human, inviting style—that he understands these painful realities, as he says, from the inside out. He knows what it is like to experience not only the symptoms of bipolar disorder but also the many reasons people put off getting help, or get the wrong kind of help. In this book, he tells his personal story candidly, with great courage and with the aim of shedding light on the world of mental illnesses and on showing the path to controlled, happy, productive living.

Among the most important messages he reveals is this one: Through denial, confusion, or embarrassment, an individual who might be bipolar can spend unhappy, turbulent years avoiding taking the first step to finding the answers he needs. And that first step might be as simple—or as hard—as talking to his doctor about what's been going on.

As a family practitioner, I have been Paul's doctor for a number of years. In one of the following chapters, he tells a little about the time he first spoke to me about the difficulties he was having and about the decisions and actions that followed that day and brought him to his current healthy state. Though I am not a specialist in mental health issues or treatment, I would comfortably and confidently add the following thoughts to Paul's experience and good advice.

If you are worried about periods of depression or manic behaviors, if you are not sure why you are the way you are, take the first step: Call your doctor, make an appointment, go in and talk. Many people find the prospect of hunting up psychiatric help to be daunting and unpleasant, but you can simply start with your family doctor, general practitioner, or internist. Don't be afraid or ashamed to tell the truth about your concerns. Know that this professional has almost certainly heard all kinds of stories. He or she should be willing to spend enough time with you to listen to your whole, honest story, without sounding judgmental or disapproving. He or she should point you toward a physician with expertise in the diagnosis and treatment of bipolar disorder. And a good physician will learn from you as well, and be grateful for the experience.

The Up and Down Life will give you support in this effort, from one who knows; it will also give you great hope for the future and a few laughs as well. Paul has spent much of his life making people laugh, and his talents as a stand-up comic and public speaker enliven these pages. They enable him to present a unique and welcome perspective on what it's like to live with bipolar disorder. Many individuals come to define themselves as their illness. The better path—the mentally healthier path—is to view it as an aspect of the self and, when possible, even to find a bit of humor from time to time.

Finally, Paul most powerfully conveys here the idea that anyone with bipolar disorder—anyone, in fact, who is living with a chronic illness that must be carefully managed and controlled—needs to take responsibility for his successes. Good medicine, and that includes proper diagnosis, treatment, and follow-up, goes only so far. Only those who fully embrace a commitment to their own well-being reap the full benefits. In his detailed account of the many ways he takes responsibility for his health, including admissions of the occasional all-too-human slip-up, Paul outlines workable ideas for all readers.

This is a book written by a man with a good heart, an indomitable spirit, and hard-won life lessons he is willing and eager to share in order to help others.

—Steve Winhusen, M.D.

Who Is Paul E. Jones, and Why Is He Telling You All This?

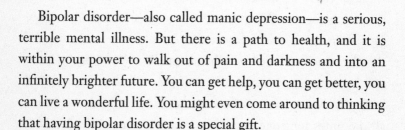

Bipolar disorder—also called manic depression—is a serious, terrible mental illness. But there is a path to health, and it is within your power to walk out of pain and darkness and into an infinitely brighter future. You can get help, you can get better, you can live a wonderful life. You might even come around to thinking that having bipolar disorder is a special gift.

And I know what I'm talking about.

So allow me to introduce myself:

Let me say right off the bat, though I have written this book about mental illness, a medical condition, I am not a doctor and I have never played one on TV. I'm a musician and songwriter. I had a stand-up comedy career for about seventeen years. I produce commercials. Of late, I've also been doing a lot of public speaking about mental illness, and that is now my main focus. How I got there is kind of interesting.

Several years ago, I came to the point of wanting to end my own life. After sitting down for seven or eight hours and writing my suicide letter, I found that I had actually talked myself into living some more. Later, I was persuaded to publish this letter as a short book. It was my attempt to explain the experiences, the thoughts, the misery that brought me to considering suicide. At the time, I had recently been diagnosed with bipolar disorder—after twenty-six years of not knowing what the hell was going on with me, except that I was a kind of raving lunatic sometimes and so depressed other times that I could hardly move. This diagnosis—at last, a name to what was wrong—was a relief on one hand; on the other hand, I was still in a very dark place.

After the book came out, to my surprise I began getting calls to speak before small groups—a college organization here, a hospital staff there—and I accepted these requests. I was amazed! People actually wanted to hear about this mental health thing, and in particular, my somewhat off-the-wall take on the whole issue. All those years of believing I needed to hide my symptoms, all the times someone said, "Just tone it down, don't let anyone know you're having problems or you'll lose gigs"—and now, I was discovering there was an audience for what I had to say. Not only that, but in short time organizations and groups actually paid me to come and tell my story.

Wow! In addition to making a little money, I began to notice something rather unexpected. People came up to me and told me I was changing their lives. I started receiving letters saying "your talk saved me, thank you." From individuals who were married to or otherwise living with people who battled the demon of depression, I heard that my words had helped them understand, for the first time, what a loved one was feeling. Another wow! All the lost years, the darkness, the mania in my life, all of it in some strange way had been leading me up to this point. There was a reason or a purpose I could discern. And that bolstered my belief that I have something useful to convey.

I have talked now to thousands of people, both bipolar sufferers themselves and their loving family members and friends. It's a two-way dialogue, not only during my in-person visits to groups and organizations around the country, but through my website (www.bipolarsurvivor.com), where folks can ask me questions and offer their own opinions. A recent venture is my weekly talk radio show, *Speaking of Life, with Paul Jones*, where the dialogue continues.

I've listened to what these men and women have to say, what worries them and what encourages them. I've learned a huge amount from them all, and I came to some conclusions that formed the shape and the message of the book I wanted to write— the book you have in your hands. Here are just a few of those conclusions:

- Too many people who have the symptoms of our illness do not go for help, or put off going for help for way too long, or get the wrong *kind* of help for way too long.

- People who are at last correctly diagnosed get not enough information or wrong information about what's coming up next, what they can expect as they start treatment, and what they can expect in the years ahead.

- People with bipolar disorder often feel weird, strange, and alone. They feel stigmatized and looked at as "crazy."

I know where these folks are coming from! I have been there! In some ways, I am still there or still finding the need to fight the same battles every day.

And so: *An Up and Down Life*. I'm excited that I've written it, I'm excited that it has been published, and I'm absolutely thrilled that you have it—because I believe I will be able to arm you with the truth, or at least some truths you're not hearing elsewhere. You will not find here another two hundred pages of medical information and opinion. Medical information has its place, but it doesn't tell the whole story. I want to pick up where a lot of "official" accounts drop off, to fill in the blanks. I set out to write a book that someone like myself will read and say, "Yes! It's about doggone time somebody told it like this!"

We who have the mental illness of bipolar disorder get better in various ways or through various routes, including, first and foremost, getting a proper diagnosis and getting the right medication. But we also get better—and stay on that good track—by telling our stories, sharing our experiences, and reminding each other what we're up against. So this book is largely my story, or stories.

You'll also read here stories from a lot of other people. Many of them are folks who came to one of my talks and spoke up, describing what it has been like for them to live with bipolar disorder. From them, I uncovered a lot of those blanks that need to be filled in—what questions aren't being answered, what issues aren't being addressed, what surprises pop up in the course of treatment. Their quoted words form the titles for my chapters. To protect their privacy, I have changed identifying names, details, or characteristics, while maintaining the core truths of their experiences.

I look at everything I do as being in the entertainment business, which is what blessedly prevents me from having to put on a tie and be nice to people and do things I don't care much about. When I go out on the road now, it's partly for the same reason really as when I was performing my comedy shows—to make people feel better, to cheer them up, and to offer them hope along with a laugh or two.

I should warn you that I'm not always so polite. When I give one of my talks, there's usually one or two folks who are taken aback by what I have to say, or at least by the way that I say it. It is odd, I suppose, to listen to stories about suicide and other disturbing topics and find yourself laughing, and then maybe crying a little, and laughing again. Doesn't seem quite proper, maybe. But I open every talk in the same way; I say, "If you are overly politically correct, you probably should leave now and go to the bathroom for about an hour." Because I want to feel free to speak the truth about this illness, without worrying a whole lot about whether I'll offend some sensitive soul out there in my audience.

Introduction

As you read *An Up and Down Life*, I'm hoping you will be a little entertained, maybe find a few laughs. Sometimes we need to lighten up and see the humor in our "crazy" lives.

Putting it all together on these pages, I have conveyed, I hope, the full flavor of a bipolar journey, what it's like from the inside. I am also hoping you will take away good ideas about walking the path, and also some comfort in the struggle to find support and stay well. None of us can ever really walk in another's shoes. But we can get a glimpse, and maybe the glimpses you'll get here look familiar. Maybe they will shed light on what you're going through. Most of all, they will show, I think, the uniqueness and the sameness of living a life with bipolar disorder. This *is* a lonely illness, but we who have it are not alone. We have each other to share our stories, give our warnings, convey our revelations, and relate our triumphs.

ONE

"You Move from the Dark into the Light"

Getting on the Path to Getting Better

"*I am a designer. I make one-of-a-kind women's patchwork coats and knitted sweaters, which I sell in specialty shops in two major cities. I'm a creative, witty, intelligent, and imaginative kind of person, and a caring person with a great capacity to love.*

"*Before I learned about this illness, I lived in hell for many, many years. Sometimes flying ridiculously high, sometimes crashing. Two short-lived, equally ill-conceived marriages. A suicide attempt. I saw a lot of doctors. I was on various medications at various times that didn't work or made things worse. If I did not have my craft, my talent, God knows what would have happened, because I was functionally unemployable in a normal job. I just kept thinking, If only I knew why. Why was I the way I was? Why did I feel this way?*"

Rachel, thirty-five, wrote those words after finally being

accurately diagnosed. Finally, she said, she had the answer to her question. And she's getting the help she needs. "You move, literally, out of hell," she said. "You move from the dark into the light."

Rachel is one and I am another of the approximately two million adults in the United States who have bipolar disorder. I'm way too familiar with the years of hell and the need to find the *why*. But most of all, best of all, I've learned so much about getting better and what it requires, and that's what this book is all about. Getting better is unquestionably walking a path, one with surprises and pitfalls, as well as joys and even some splendid possibilities along the way, and forever.

First, my hat's off to Rachel. I don't know her well, and yet I do know her, in a way. I have no doubt that she correctly describes herself as creative, imaginative, intelligent, caring. That's part and parcel of this disorder. That's part of the deal. Let me toot our bipolar horn for a moment. The drive, the courage, the intensity of feeling, all that is very common in people who have manic depression, and all that makes this not only a challenge but a gift that can produce a splendid outcome. A man who was wrongly diagnosed for many years wrote, "My life has been both wonderful and tragic." In these pages, I want to show how to get at the wonderful, which is a bipolar life under control, a life in the light. And it can be done, absolutely. I can say today, I wouldn't trade my life for anyone's. Maybe you'll say the same.

Bipolar disorder is a mental illness, a mood disorder characterized by manic periods and depressed periods. During a manic episode, which can go on for a few hours, a week, or months, your mood is elevated, expansive, and grandiose, with racing thoughts, little need for sleep, and maybe a lot of wild risk taking. During a depressed phase, you are, well, depressed—sad, hopeless, maybe paralyzed into inactivity. That, roughly, is the official description, and it's pretty accurate, though I have a few refinements to make later.

What does it feel like to have bipolar disorder? Here's what I have heard from some of the brave folks who have shared their stories:

"There's the sense that you can't inhabit your own skin, you're jumping out of it. You are irritable, crabby, a witch to anyone who comes near you."

"It's being so down that you can't even cry. How bad is that, that you wish you could have a good cry, and you can't?"

"I was on hyperalert; things get heightened—sounds, colors, people. I would get extremely paranoid and rather mean to people. Then I'd feel blissfully happy again."

"Have you ever sat in a room full of people at a party and tried to listen to every single conversation going on? And tried to actually participate in each one of those conversations? That's how it would get for me, except I was the only person in the room and the conversations were going on in my head, and I was attempting to keep up with each thought and complete each thought."

"Depression is a mental thing, but it hits your whole body. It was as if I had not enough strength to lift my arms or move my legs."

Yeah, there's a little taste of what it's like.

This book is set up as kind of the before and after picture, "before" referring to the uncontrolled, unstabilized bipolar experience and "after" referring to the time following diagnosis, getting medicated, and getting on track. The before and after aren't actually all that clear-cut, for the simple reason that you are not cured of this illness, ever. It's always with you. Nevertheless, the before and after can look, and should look, very different. It's a matter of moving from the dark into the light.

Throughout this book, but especially in the next two chapters, I want to paint the before picture. This is the full flavor of untreated bipolar disorder that I promised you, and I think it's very important to spell it out in all its grimness, and a little bit of its glory, because people who haven't been there don't get it. Hell, if you have this illness yourself, *you* may not get it, or not for a long time. One of the reasons is that bipolar behavior can be misunderstood, minimized, or dismissed by everyone as "the normal" carried just a little too far. Isn't life just naturally full of highs and lows? Doesn't everyone feel sometimes euphoric and sometimes down in the dumps? Aren't we all a tad bipolar?

People who don't have it may decide it feels like nothing, because they don't quite believe it exists. Or bipolar behavior may just seem to them annoying, bizarre, or self-indulgent. But "highs and lows" and "ups and downs" barely give an idea of what may be going on, from bursts of great accomplishment and wide-awakeness to rages and temper flare-ups, from feelings of overwhelming persecution or generosity to black despair and immobility.

Another of the reasons people don't get it is that some stuff associated with this disorder is desirable and intriguing. We say now, well, this is obviously what so many brilliant artists and musicians and talented folks had, and they wouldn't have been all that brilliant and talented if they weren't bipolar. There is probably truth in that observation. Certainly, I'd put money on the fact that 85 percent of the most creative, spontaneous, tremendously smart, wickedly funny people I've run into over my checkered career in the entertainment business had bipolar traits.

However—and here's the big "however"—we must keep our eye on the downside. That is, both manic and depressive episodes can cause immense damage and suffering. They can cause you to lose your family or your job or your home. Or they can kill you. So I offer the full flavor. Read about the before picture. This is what bipolar disorder looks like, sounds like, feels like. It is critical that both we who live with this illness and those family and friends who are trying to live with *us* know the score.

And then we get into the after picture, which must begin with getting accurately diagnosed. Sounds like that should not be a huge problem. Wrong. It is a huge problem. *Research studies tell us that about two-thirds of bipolar sufferers in the United States have not been correctly diagnosed or are not seeking or receiving proper treatment.* This is a tragedy for a lot of reasons, not least of all because about 20 percent of those individuals will commit suicide.

So accurate diagnosis is key. How do you get one? I have a lot to say later about the often thorny, infuriating path to locating a good doctor and then working with that individual in the most productive way. Some medical professionals—psychologists, psychiatrists—are great. Some are clueless. Some don't have time to pay attention, or they're uninterested. The ball is in your court in fighting for the answers you need. I will arm you in chapter 4 with the questions you should be asking, the answers you should be hearing, and the information you need. Get the right help and the right treatment, as early as you can.

People diagnosed with bipolar disorder are almost always put on medication. And now your path to getting well takes an interesting turn. A common misconception is that starting with the pills is the end of your troubles. What I have learned, from my own medicated experience and from hearing the stories of so many others, is that in some ways the game is about to begin. The pills are great; they can be, literally, lifesavers. But there's a lot you should know about beginning a medication regimen and what it takes to stick with it. The temptations *not* to stick with it can be strong, and in chapter 5, I'll explain just what those are and how to avoid them. Side effects are no fun. Feeling lousier than you did before you started with the pills is certainly no fun, and hugely discouraging. But when you know what to expect, you are prepared. You recognize these as temporary bumps in the road or steps along the path.

And then what else do you need? There's so much you can do for yourself to stay well, and mostly it's not rocket science. We need to try, as best we can, to live in a healthful way—eat right, sleep right, shape up, all those behaviors that really are good for anyone, sick or not. In chapter 6, on self-monitoring and self-regulation, we look at why all that good stuff is doubly important for us bipolars.

A terrific thing that happens with the people who are most

successfully walking the path of wellness, I have discovered, is that they come to "read" their moods very clearly—the signs that they're maybe starting to get a little too hyper or a little too down—and they take corrective actions to head off a cycling episode. And they do this without making a huge federal case out of it all, which helps them get better a little more. Living with bipolar disorder should be kind of like living with diabetes, something to take seriously, but not let define your life. So in that chapter I also offer some thoughts on your environment—who's in it and who maybe should not be. I think you have to decontaminate your life, as far as possible, by steering clear of people and places that are just not great for you to be around.

The caring and concerned support people in a bipolar's life—spouse, mom, dad, brother, sister, great and good friend—are the salt of the earth. I have met so many of them, and I stand in admiration of these folks who are trying to be helpful in all kinds of ways. It's no easy job. Sometimes, they don't know exactly what being helpful involves—what to say, what not to say, how to be encouraging without being pushy or intrusive or overly controlling. I will share in chapter 7 some ideas for the support team, including what might be the most important part of the job—keeping a lid on things when the bipolar loved one is possibly heading into a slightly manic episode.

Speaking before groups has opened up a new world to me, and one thing I have learned is that many, many people are struggling with mental illness of one kind or another—and not enough attention is being paid. Not enough is being done to improve their lives. Hey, our leaders do not have to pass a mental evaluation to run the country, yet I could not get a security clearance anymore to clean the toilets in the White House. I cannot buy life insurance for my family. That is the stigma that comes with mental illness, and that's something we need to erase. So educating others about bipolar disorder—explaining and demonstrating that having a bio-chemical imbalance of the brain does not mean you are a weird, scary, dangerous person—is part of helping us all get better, I believe.

But on a personal, individual level, who do you tell and who do you not tell? Is informing someone you know that you are being treated for a mental illness educating that person into greater wisdom, or is it courting disaster or at least embarrassment for yourself? So many people I talk to feel compelled to say nothing, to stay under the radar. Sometimes that may be a smart move; sometimes it may add to your burden. In chapter 8, on educating others, I will outline some simple plans for figuring out who you should tell, who not to tell, and how to do it. Sharing the news with your sister is one thing, while telling your boss or your coworkers is obviously something else.

Finally, making peace with your unstabilized bipolar past is very important. I would go even further, and say that it is the one effort that will get you truly walking in the light again. Chapter 9 discusses making peace—forgiving yourself for some old mistakes, and you surely ran up a few of those; getting in touch with people you blew off or avoided or were mean to during your sick days, and offering an explanation and maybe an apology; living better today—it's all part of healing and stepping out boldly on the next leg of the journey.

Here's the bottom line:

You are the only one who can take the right actions. No one else is going to handle this thing for you. You must know what is going on in your mind and in your body. Bipolar disorder is real, it is strong, and it is very sneaky, a bitch to live with, certainly. I have to be more real, more strong, and teach myself to outfox the fox. So do you. At the same time, paradoxically, it can bring with it gifts—of creativity and imagination, of insight, of empathy for our human condition, of kindness and understanding for people who are "different," of talents and energy. Gifts we should embrace.

TWO

"Like a Seesaw Being Pushed by Some Giant, Crazy Hand"

What It Feels Like to Have Bipolar Disorder

A bipolar friend of mine made the comparison to being on a seesaw, and it's a good one. You're up and down, up and down, and where you stop, nobody knows, but look out below, because when you land, it's going to cause a ruckus. When I was sick, I was up and down sometimes four, five times in a day. High as a kite without the ingestion of any drug or drink. There was not a problem that I did not have the answer to, nothing I could not fix; I was the guy everyone could count on to get the job done. So I believed. Then, as fast as the seesaw went up, down it came. Just a day earlier or a few minutes earlier I was ready to take on the world, and there I was now, not even capable of deciding if I should have something to eat or jump out a window.

The seesaw had no middle ground for me. It was driving me

crazy, controlling my life, and though I knew I didn't want to play this game anymore, I couldn't figure out how to get off.

Do you know what I'm talking about? Have you been there?

This illness is a shock to live with; it has so many faces, so many different ways of tearing your heart out of your body, and yet most people looking on probably have no idea what you're going through. You may not really get it either.

The medical profession has a lot to say about the faces of bipolar disorder these days, and thank God they do. At the same time, the medical description, as expressed in many books and official websites and the like, tends to tie it all up a little too neatly, in my opinion: here are the symptoms of mania, here are the symptoms of depression, here are the warning signs, here's what we mean by bipolar I and bipolar II, and so on. In reality, in its untreated state this is a really messy illness that's not all so tidy and explainable. Which is one reason I believe the best medical professional to diagnose you is one who himself or herself lives with the disorder (more on that score in chapter 4), because that's going to be someone who understands it from the inside. More in that chapter, too, about those different categories—I and II and mixed episodes and so on. To tell you the truth, the terms don't hold great significance for me. They go only so far in conveying the full flavor of the bipolar life.

Bipolar disorder will attack each one of us in a special, weird, and crazy way. Rapid cycling—the up to down to up to down again in the space of a day—is something I experienced many times, but it's not the main way I used to live with this illness. Most of my up episodes lasted for long stretches; down episodes lingered for months; then, during the final stage of my undiagnosed life, I was in a depression for three and a half years without a break of any kind. I would have loved to get a good manic phase going during that period; it didn't come.

> People do look at you funny when you drive standing up behind the wheel of your convertible. One lady actually screamed to me, "You're standing up." Like I didn't know that.

But being in a depressive state can actually create issues similar to the manic side of the illness, which is why I say this is not all so neat and tidy. I could not get out of that depression no matter what I tried, and I tried a lot of stuff. Risk taking? Reckless behavior without worrying about the consequences? You bet. Spending money wildly and unwisely was one thing, having two affairs was another—and I was a married man with a wonderful wife and three great kids. I'd drive my car standing up, with the top down, or careen around on my motorcycle while kind of hanging off the back, behind the seat. I hadn't yet made up my mind to take my life, but I was living so that it would be taken from me.

I would say that many people who live on the edge like that don't really care if they stay or go. That's what gives you the courage or whatever it is to do the stupid stuff, to be the daredevil. When you're in such a state that nothing matters, the only thing you become attached to is stopping the physical and mental pain, in any way you can. That's right, I said physical pain. You know the commercials, "Depression hurts." I hate those commercials. I do not know why, but I do. Oh, what the hell, I do know why: because it reminds me of just how damn bad being depressed physically did hurt. I know of people who literally cut themselves with a razor blade on their arms, legs, and stomachs in an effort to let the pain out of their bodies. I have never gone that far—I hate the sight of blood, plus I like the way my body looks without the scars. I have enough of those in my mind. The pain of depression can come in many forms. For me, my body would hurt so bad that I thought I was filled with tumors. At times my head felt so filled it would take everything I had not to stick something in my ear to get the pain out.

Your mental health can play a huge role in your physical health and well-being. There is a pain associated with it. How severe, I think, depends on the person.

In this chapter, I want to share a few stories from the time before I got to a good doctor and before I got a diagnosis, the time I was terribly ill. I'll put my face on bipolar disorder, and maybe you will recognize something of yourself. Maybe you will see here some of the features that we share, each in our own fashion.

The Sad, Mad, and Sick King of Comedy: My Story

In my twenties, married, a father, I was trying to be a responsible guy, working in a business with some family members and making money. And despite having these people I loved in my life, despite the money, I couldn't stand much of anything, so an old friend and I put together our former band, started practicing, and went out playing in bars for about fifty dollars each a night. Within about six months, I realized that sucked. I enjoyed playing the music, but did not enjoy the bars and the drunks. One evening a patron decided to throw up on my speakers and *I* decided that did it for me and the rock and roll life. That same night someone suggested I sign up for an open mike night at a place called the Funny Bone Comedy Club, a thought that had not occurred to me before, but the next day I got a date to do a show, and about two weeks later I went up onstage for the first time.

Wow! I rocked! Yes, the crowd loved me, *I* loved me, no drunks threw up on my stuff, and I was the king of comedy! This was the way to go, baby, one man, one stage. After the show, a bunch of us "open mikers" went next door to the bar to talk about how great we were, and I was trying to get all the answers to all the new questions all of a sudden racing through my head: Who do I talk to about getting a TV show? How long does it take before you're famous? When do I get a dressing room? I will be in my trailer, I want all the green M&M's removed from that bowl. . . . Yes indeed, comedy was it for me.

Let me switch metaphors now from the seesaw to the roller coaster. Little did I know that I was about to jump on the biggest roller-coaster ride of my life, one that would last for the next eleven years. Little did I know that this one night onstage would end up costing me a fortune and at the same time save my life.

Here's what I mean by that last statement. Comedy allowed me to be who I was. I could say or do anything I wanted to, anything that was legal, and get away with it. If I wanted to call a fat lady fat, I called her fat. If I wanted to tell a Catholic joke, I told the joke. Need to call someone a dumb hick hillbilly? Do it! And still get paid! I got away with a lot of this stuff not only onstage but offstage, because once people knew I was Paul Jones, Stand-Up

Comic, I had permission to be as rude and obnoxious as I pleased. Stand-up comedy might be the single best job in the world for someone with this illness. When I was angry, I had the stage; when I was sad, when I was manic, I had the stage. No matter what, I could express my moods without fear of getting fired. I'm not saying this is all very nice. Rude, obnoxious, insulting is not nice. But I am absolutely certain doing comedy is why I did not end up in the hospital or in jail. It saved my life—for a while.

It wasn't long before I left the business I'd been in with my brothers and, in my late twenties, headed out to be a full-time comic. That first year, I did 198 shows, driving maybe fifteen hours to get to one. Started writing a lot of music again as well, just going to concentrate on being my creative self, maybe not be a rock and roller anymore but I could sure write some songs and shop them in Nashville. Life was great, right? Not!

I wasn't in a total funk, but around this time I was cycling very fast through mania and depression. Around this time, too, is when I unconsciously began trying to do away with myself, and I had a few routes by which that could happen. First was the crazy driving in the car. Second was the alcohol route. My drinking had become very, very bad, only when I was on the road. I was literally trying to kill myself with alcohol, coming to under sinks in hotel rooms, waking up praying for help—which I didn't think I deserved. But I'd arrive back home and be there for a month, not have a drink for thirty days, and not have a problem with that. Because I had made a promise to myself and to my wife when we had our kids that they'd never see me drunk. I stuck by that promise. So I stayed gone as much as I could, maybe, just so I could drink, and because I knew that something was terribly wrong with me. Spinning out of control.

Meanwhile, comedy was taking good care of me. And this is where another route to oblivion came in. In my act, I would push and push people, trying like hell to offend them just to see what would happen. Maybe if I pissed off the right person, one who happened to have a gun, I'd get shot, which is actually what I was going for. I understand that now. It's sort of like suicide-by-cop, which is when a guy gets the cops to kill him because he doesn't want to do it himself. My version was suicide-by-fan, or something like that. It never happened. I'd be onstage, being mean as hell, and get a standing ovation at the end of my show. In all those years, no one ever even tried to beat me up.

So comedy was a lifesaver. But it was also a kind of cage. No matter how I was feeling, I always seemed to be alone, checking into a hotel somewhere and not coming out until it was time to do my show. The road is a lonely place. Eventually, I sensed that my family got used to me being gone, or I convinced myself that they had, and that's when my drinking and self-destructiveness started to get really bad. On the road, I just wanted to be home with my wife and kids, safe in my own bed. When I did get home safe in my own bed, I just wanted to be on the road, headed for a hotel room. By that time, I did not belong anywhere. That's why I say comedy was a cage. It kept me safe when I needed it and it held me back when I should have been moving forward.

When I began to feel as if I was not needed by anyone, that was when I started trying my best to die and began dreaming of getting killed. I needed help pretty bad by that time. Lots of alcohol, four packs of cigarettes a day, not much in the way of decent food, filling up with sugar, I was one toxic dude walking around—and being one hell of a great comic! If I may say so myself, I was funny! Nothing was stopping anything from coming out of my mouth. I was so angry at the world that I got kicked off a number of radio stations. Which turned out to be just fine, because when there's a little something in the local paper about this wild man getting kicked off the radio, that makes even more people come out to see the crazy guy onstage.

My eleven-year roller-coaster ride. For an hour or so at night, when I stood up there making a live audience laugh, the pain *would* stop. Eventually, that relief wasn't enough. The only answer was making the whole thing stop for good.

The Chosen One

A common aspect of bipolar illness is this: At some point you begin to have an unreal spiritual experience or sense of yourself. You feel that God or a higher power of some sort has chosen you, and only you, for a mission. Something really huge. Alternating with the depression and self-destructiveness, I believed off and on that I was destined to go out and save the world, or at least affect it in some powerfully positive way that others would recognize. And if you're feeling like the chosen one, and if you happen to fall in with a couple of other people similarly touched by notions of grandiosity, there's a kind of kinetic explosion of energy that can send you far, far out into the realms of unreality.

During one doozy manic period, I was trying very hard to secure a music writing deal, realizing I was getting a little too fat and too old to keep moving on the road. Consequently, I was spending a lot of time in Nashville, driving back and forth from my home in Cincinnati many times a week, because where else can you get a deal writing dark stuff about women walking out on you and your dog running away? Hanging out with people I thought could help me, getting at least somewhat in the network of songwriters and producers, I was feeling I had a shot.

On this occasion, a February day, when I am already on a pretty good, flash-in-the-pants manic trip, I drop by the office of my friend and manager, Miles, and he introduces me to a couple of guys named Tony and Andy, not their real names. I'm disguising their identities to protect the innocent, or maybe it's the guilty, but I can tell you that even if you know nothing much about popular and country music, you will have heard about these two. Hit songs, sales in the millions, Tony and Andy separately were major players in the music industry. "Why don't you all go in the meeting room," Miles says, "get to know each other, heck, maybe you'll come up with something we can all make some money on."

So we head into the conference room, and here is where things start to get a bit goofy. The second the door shuts, the air turns a little strange. Charged. We start to talk, and Tony tells me that his new life mission is to reach kids and help them get off drugs and alcohol, tells me he and his wife are traveling from town to town, trying to change the world one child at a time. Now Andy is talking about how he is also out to change the world through his music and he's looking to get involved in something really meaningful. Immediately, I love these guys! I, too, am on a course to save the planet any way I can!

We start listening to each other's music, and we're all weeping, overcome with emotion. We're amazing, we're creative geniuses, our talents know no depth. We are all so blessed, we have all been called. At one point, we literally start arguing about who is the most blessed, who is the chosen one. "I'm God's favorite." "No, you're not, I am, He brought you to me, remember?"

Sometime in the midst of it all the whole thing went almost blank in my mind. There was no alcohol, no drugs involved that day. I remember now the three of us gathered around a little crappy tape recorder, playing our CDs, taking turns inventing lyrics and playing the guitar, and my mind and my body were actually working outside of me. It was as though I was sitting across the room on the couch, watching as we all wrote and played at the table. Three guys who felt they had a calling, being literally plugged into each other by a spiritual force.

Another knock on the door, and it's Miles, asking how we're all doing. "Man, wait till you hear this song," we all say, and there's Paul, Tony, and Andy all hugging and high-fiving each other, as though we're getting ready to unveil the *Mona Lisa*. No doubt in our minds, we have a major, world-changing record.

Magic dust fills the room. We all watch Miles as he listens, and I feel a tear coming down my cheek. Just as it's almost falling off, a chill goes straight up my back, as if I have been touched by an angel. I do not want to wipe that tear away; it feels too good. The song ends, and there are we three geniuses, grown men—having been in that room for over eighteen hours, as I learned later—sobbing out loud over a song that is actually a piece of crap, as Miles gently suggests, not using that word; a song that to this day, I could not repeat for you one line or even explain what the point of it was.

Have you ever felt tapped by a higher power as the one and only human on earth to bring love, peace, happiness, and truth to the masses? When I mention this aspect during one of my talks, there are always one or two people who I see smile a little, look down, slowly shake their heads. They recognize that we bipolars often experience that sense of grandiosity and specialness, and what follows in the wake of that is loss of perspective and the ability to reflect sanely on any of our actions.

Feeling like the chosen one led me to do some extraordinarily idiotic things, and also a few decent and generous ones. It made me inclined to hand money to people whenever they asked, for one thing. Some of that money did good; a lot of it was downright wasted, and I did learn one lesson: you don't get it back. I can safely say that I rashly burned through more than a quarter of a million dollars in five years—on the good works, partly, flying all over the country on my dime on behalf of nonprofit organizations, as I was playing out my chosen one role and searching for something to give me meaning. But there was also buying bad stocks and waiting for the big payday that never came, and buying new cars. Chalk it all up to visions of grandiosity, carelessness, dumbness, some good old-fashioned human greed, and a few admirable good intentions.

Spending money you don't have—or spending the money you *do* have recklessly—is one of the notable traits of this illness. And that can happen when you're depressed and when you're manic. I hear this all the time from the people I talk to. When they're down, they buy in a desperate effort to make themselves feel life is worth living. When they're up, they buy because they don't really know what they're doing, that cash might be Monopoly paper. Sometimes it involves a combination, feeling down and feeling up.

> I coined the phrase, "Do you accept stolen credit cards?" That always got a laugh and "Sure." Little did they know I actually felt I was using a stolen card, because I realized I couldn't afford what I was buying at the time.

Brenda, forty-two, tells this sad story about a woman and her money.

"When you talk about a woman who shops a lot, it sounds kind of funny or silly. You're a shopaholic. Like being a chocaholic, something you shouldn't do, but not so serious. I know otherwise. Excessive shopping, buying things you don't need and can in no way in this lifetime afford, is absolutely part of this disease.

"Buying stuff made me feel simultaneously elated, on a high, and sick to my stomach. I had something like twenty bank credit cards at one time. When I was feeling agitated and jumpy, I had to buy something. It was like needing your fix, what I imagine it's like to have a crack addiction or something. One night, I just kind of hit the wall with the whole thing. I remember this in vivid detail. There was a ring I saw in a shop and had to have. So I went through the whole thing of telling myself I could not have it, could not afford it, this was bad. Predictably, that didn't work for long. I was at home after work, fixing myself a little dinner, obsessing about the ring, and I ran out, jumped in a cab, and went downtown to this shop and bought the ring. Charged it. Then I jumped in another cab back to my apartment. In the taxi, I was looking at the ring—very pretty, sterling silver with a small cabochon sapphire and two tiny rubies, cost $275—and I had something like a panic attack. I started sobbing and sobbing. The taxi driver is looking in his rearview like he's got a crazy lady in his car."

That was the beginning of a long, hard stretch of time for Brenda, starting with sessions at a credit counseling agency in an attempt to establish schedules for paying off her creditors and ending with her declaration of bankruptcy.

Money cannot make bipolar disorder go away. But bipolar disorder sure can make your money go away.

The Hallucinator

Manic episodes can be exciting when they're going on; I certainly felt great sitting in that music room and writing the songs that would save the world. Or they can be terrifying, spiraling into extreme manifestations that might end in hallucinations, psychotic behavior, or hospitalization. The psychotic behavior and the hospitals were not among the faces of my bipolar picture, fortunately, but I know a thing or two about hallucinations, or whatever they should be called.

Many occurred during those times I was on my quest for the gold ring, the big-time success, driving back and forth to shows and Nashville and home, getting by for hours on end without sleep, food, or anything relatively normal.

On one such occasion, I am about three hours into a seven-hour drive, when it begins to snow, not a comforting sight if you're in a Mustang convertible. Before long, I'm driving in a total whiteout, like having a sheet over the window, and more or less lost. The windshield wipers are going like crazy, making that skitchy, jumpy sound as the rubber drags across, which drives me crazier than I already am. I am basically sticking my head out the side trying to spot some signs and find an exit. Which, at last, I do, the Mustang literally scraping the ground.

Pulling into a McDonald's parking lot, I turn off the engine and put my head on the steering wheel. The effects of this little manic episode are beginning to take a toll on my body: terrible back pain from all the hours in the car, brain getting deprived of oxygen from all the cigarettes. Walking to the restaurant, I say out loud, "God, you have to help me here, I cannot make this drive but I need the money from this show I've got to get to. Please help me."

Now here's where strange comes in. I get some food, hit the restroom, start walking back to the car, and I note that the snow is now down to a trickle, a flake here and a flake there. I'm driving out of the lot, bottom of the car still hitting snow, and by the time I'm nearing the entrance ramp to the highway, I see something very odd. All the snow is melted. The snow on the road, on the grass, all of it is gone, like it never happened. The landscape is dry as a bone.

If I'd told anybody about that little scene right then, that individual would surely have sent the people in white jackets out after me. I remember driving on, talking to myself about what had happened, and at the time in my mind it was without a doubt an act of God, his way of making sure my family would be able to eat and I'd be able to pay my bills. That's the explanation I still prefer to keep, instead of searching for a scientific one. Or instead of considering that the whole thing—the snow and the disappearance of the snow—was a reflection of my distorted mental state. A hallucination. A figment of my bizarre imagination.

During another occasion, again on the road, I'm heading out after a show in New York City, heading back to Nashville in the (pathetically delusional) belief that I've got a major music deal there just waiting for me. At this point my mind is not only sick because I'm sick, which I don't know, but sick from no sleep, no food. Confused. My head is spinning, I'm spinning. I need a boost, and nothing works better than a good old-fashioned manic illusion. I'm going to be rich beyond my wildest dreams— awesome! I am back in the saddle. Manic magic, here I come.

I'm told I should take the Lincoln Tunnel to get out of New York and onto an interstate that will lead me to Nashville, a roughly 930-mile trip. Predictably, we sit in the tunnel for what seems to be forever, and sitting there, feeling the fumes melt away whatever is left of my oxygen, I begin to wonder just what it is I am trying to prove or do. Even though I am in the middle of a pretty strong manic phase, I am still, occasionally, able to realize that I'm pushing the envelope. Short-lived, sane glimpses of reality do pop into my head. And I think: Is this yet another wild chase of fame, or is it the real deal? Will Lisa be home when I get there eventually, or will she have finally made a wise choice and left? Yes, I am able to recognize that my wife should probably take off and start living a somewhat normal life, because this way of functioning has got to be taking a toll on her. At this time still, there was no diagnosis, and therefore no illness to point to. This was simply life with Paul, and how much fun could that possibly be?

Then traffic in the tunnel starts moving, the glimpses of sanity disappear, the rush comes back—time to get this train rolling again. As the end of the tunnel gets closer and closer, my eyes are getting heavier and heavier, my head is nodding, and the sounds in the car are becoming almost like a dream sequence in a movie. Thank God for those little bumpy things on the side of the road, the bumps that when you hit them make your heart leap up into your throat. And thank God that one of my fellow travelers through that tunnel is not ready for me to ruin his or her day, and gives a loud horn honk to further snap my head up and keep me in my lane.

Now here's the really loopy part of this little manic story.

I close my eyes, suddenly hear and feel the open air whoosh through the car signaling that I have cleared the tunnel, and so I open my eyes. I'm approaching a highway sign, and written on it is "Harrisburg, PA, 5 miles." As it happens, Harrisburg is about 160 miles or so from New York, or almost three hours, give or take. I smack myself in the face a couple of times. What just happened? Did I fall asleep at the wheel and the car drove itself for three hours? I am now laughing hysterically, starting to hyperventilate, losing all sense of reality and unable to stop it from happening. Did I have an accident? What if I crashed in the tunnel, and that horn I heard was me getting smacked by another car? Okay, I'm dead, that's the only explanation for what is going on here. Great, here I am dead, and for eternity I'm going to have to drive in my car. No bright lights, no heavenly gates, no nothing, I have died and I'm driving through the Lincoln Tunnel forever. On the other hand, I *am* the chosen one, or one of the chosen ones, so maybe God has picked up me and my car and brought me closer to where I have to get, to make my big score.

That's what it's like. You become lost, very lost, as life passes by and you cannot catch onto one single thing to hold you down. You cannot discern what is real and what is not.

In the Despair Beyond Despair

Those are the words William Styron used in his great book about his profound battle with depression. They're good words, because they suggest the impossible-to-describe flavor of clinical depression, impossible to describe to those who haven't been caught in its grip. You know what it's like to feel despair? This is worse.

When I speak before a group, for an organization such as the National Alliance for the Mentally Ill, I often ask the audience to tell me by a show of hands who has been depressed in their lives. And what is the feeling like? Here is when it will get interesting. Typically, the room is composed of three sorts of people: first, the consumers (crazy people like me); second, their families (support people, such as spouses and other relatives, the "normal," unsick people); and third, professionals (crazier people than all of us; just kidding, sort of). Consequently, I get a variety of answers to my question.

The "normal" people will describe depression by using words

such as "sad" . . . "unhappy" . . . "lost" . . . "really down." I might explore a little further and ask someone why he or she was depressed at some point in the past, what caused it. He or she says something like: "My father died." "I lost my job and I didn't think I'd ever get another one." "I was falling behind in my bills." "My girlfriend left me." All legitimate descriptions of being depressed and recognizable reasons for feeling so.

When I hear from the crazy people like me, they will describe depression in such a way that if I let my emotions get to me, I will begin to cry right where I stand. Why? Because I've been there. I know in my bones the particular hell they are talking about, the days upon days and the nights upon nights when life is nothing but a black hole. As they share their stories, I admire the courage it takes to re-create the experience of those days and nights, even from a distance. It's hard. The depression of this illness is so dark at times that when I considered writing this section, I did everything in my power to delay it. Too busy, have to get myself in the right frame of mind, and so on and so forth. The real reason for my procrastination was fear of what I would cause myself to remember.

The manic stuff, strange as it sounds, most of the time can be recalled somewhat with good thoughts, or maybe humorous thoughts. When it comes to depression, none of that is true. There's nothing to enjoy in retrospect, or even to remotely feel like remembering.

Think of walking into a cave, deeper and deeper, and you look back and can still see a spot of light way down at the opening. Go even deeper, hit a bend, look back, and now you see nothing. No light at all, barely any sound except for your heart beating and that god-awful noise in your head. You may know what I'm talking about, the god-awful noise. It sounds almost like bones rubbing together in your head and neck, hard to describe.

Someone without this illness doesn't get that. Depression of this kind, *when there is no apparent reason*, is written off as weakness. Self-pity. "It's all in your head." On the other hand, if your father died or you lost your job, you're allowed to be depressed—for a while. There's a kind of "acceptable depression chart" that tells us how long is long enough. Lose your dad or your sister: acceptable depression time is one year. After one year, your friends will start talking behind your back, or maybe even to you, about how it's necessary to "move forward, get on with your life." Get fired or downsized from your job, and you're allotted about three months to mope around and be miserable. If after three months you're still crying about what happened to you, you're written off as a whiny little person. If you're still in a funk six months later, now your friends and family are saying they can see why you lost your job in the first place.

Nowhere on the chart is time allowed for being depressed when there's no reason that can be seen by the naked eye. Zero depression policy.

As I mentioned earlier, during a three-year stretch right before I finally got help I was sunk in one long, deep depression that had many chapters but no end, no relief. Previously, I'd been used to rolling from manic to depressed to being somewhat normal, back to depressed and manic again all in the course of a few days, weeks, or months. Now it was just the black hole. Eventually, it became clear to me that this abyss was not going away, there would be no manic episode to snap me out of it and get me back in the game of life, at least for a little while. I knew I was sinking very fast, and though I had people around me, there was no one I felt I could turn to at this point. I can see now that I should have died then for sure.

Again, this was a period when I was constantly on the road, trying hard to get record deals and write hit songs. But my trips were taking on another flavor. Now I was going away from my family not to earn money, but to be alone. A certain Quality Inn in Nashville had become my home. This place had everything I needed: a bed, shower, toilet, and, most important, a bar. I'd check in simply to sleep and drink. I was never a loud, messy drinker. To the contrary, I'd buy bottles of wine, cases of beer, hole up quietly in my room, and never leave.

My hotel room always stayed dark and cold. No matter what the temperature outside, my private little supply of air was turned way down as far as it would go. I was, indeed, a bat in a cave, or at least I wanted to be one, lying in the bed with the covers pulled up over my head so as to shut out all light. The TV was on, but I'd just listen to the sound, preferring not to look out at all if possible. Sticking my head up just for a drink. Holed up there drinking to die. Not dying to drink, but drinking to die.

On this day I'm remembering now, or rather, this stretch of days, I'd come to from time to time, head pounding from the wine. Personally, I believe there's nothing worse than a wine hangover, and it's even worse when you drink so much you think you'll die and then instead of dying, you actually wake up—pissed to still be alive. Head pounding, mouth dry, eyes as red as the wine that made them that way, I'd walk into the bathroom and look at myself in the mirror. I can see my face now. A grown man with a good family, wonderful kids, a wife who'd do anything for me, and there I was in my underwear with red eyes and a pounding headache, mad as hell that I was alive.

The phone rings and it's the front desk: "Mr. Jones, will you be staying with us another day?"

Me, probably sounding like the devil himself with my voice raspy from all the booze and cigarettes: "What? What time is it?"

"It is eleven thirty in the morning and that is checkout time. Will you be staying another night?"

Me: "What day is it?" I have to ask, because I haven't opened the curtains in a long, long time, and I don't, you could say, have my bearings.

"Today is Thursday, sir."

I tell the front desk guy I'll be leaving, sorry, overslept, need a late checkout, I'll be out by noon. Run back into the bathroom, jump in the shower.

I remember now as if it was yesterday standing there while the water ran down my face and body. Did you know that when you stand under running shower water, if you try hard enough you can see a waterfall? Hear the rush as the water runs over your ears? Did you also know that when you are a grown man, standing in the shower in a hotel room that—you've just learned—you have been in for over four days, allowing the water to run down your face and pretending it's a waterfall, eventually you will realize that you are a grown man standing in the shower of a hotel room that you've been in for four days without knowing it—and that thought will make you cry like a baby?

Soon, you begin to wonder what is water from the shower and what is water from your tears. Soon, you feel as though every bit of that water is coming out of you, tears pouring from your body by the gallons. Because you're so sad that you are a grown man in a hotel room that you have been in for four lost days, a man with a wife, three kids, a dog, a man wishing he was dead and not knowing why he wished he was dead, crying tears by the gallon.

How long I was in the shower I'm not sure. I do know that I checked out of that hotel not at noon but at six thirty that night. I do know that as I drove home I could not look at myself in the mirror, because a grown man who stands in a shower in a hotel room he's been in for four days without realizing it has no right to see who he is. Four days were gone because I did not want to ask for help. Four days of not seeing my children or hugging my wife because I was afraid. That was when I reached the bottom of my personal pit.

Depression: the dictionary says things like despair, sadness, melancholy, misery. That doesn't quite cover it. It's the despair beyond despair, the misery beyond misery. To me, one word takes care of it: hell.

During all those roller-coaster years I wanted to have the answer to the question why. Not why was I doing the nutty things I was doing, but why did I feel the way I felt? Finally I got my answer. Before moving on to the "after" picture, a little exploration of the roots and causes of bipolar disorder.

THREE

"Is This What Was Wrong with My Uncle?"

Family Connections, Predispositions, and Other Vulnerabilities

When people first hear about bipolar disorder or get diagnosed with it, they naturally want to know how it got there—when did it start, what caused it, who's to blame.

Do you inherit it, like curly hair or long legs?

Is this what was wrong with you when you were a kid, though nobody had a clue, least of all you?

Does it have anything to do with drinking or smoking or being too fat?

Does stress in your life bring on symptoms?

It's one of the maddening aspects of this illness that there are no simple answers to any of these questions. The answers tend to be a mix of "yes and no," "sometimes," and "could be." They also get into the whole which-came-first-the-chicken-or-the-egg thing—are you sick because you're drinking a lot or are you drinking a lot because you're sick? My focus regarding bipolar disorder, always, is not so much where does it come from, as what are you going to do about it? Nevertheless, to be in charge of controlling our illness, to outfox the fox, it's a good idea to understand as much as we can about these roots and causes and vulnerabilities. And especially over the past couple of decades, medical people and researchers have made big strides in zeroing in on and refining some of these issues.

Understanding can put a lot into perspective, for one thing, and perspective should never be underrated.

Those of us who are most successfully functioning and managing through a bipolar life have typically spent some time tracing back, figuring out the connections and the twists and turns. You may find yourself remembering your childhood or teenaged self with greater insight.

Maybe you will recognize that a beloved but infuriating or scary or really nutty family member was or is struggling with some of the same troubles you know so well. This is real. Studies tell us that among bipolar individuals, about *20 percent of immediate relatives* have or did have a mood disorder. In my own case, I will stick my neck out and say that my family is filled with this illness, but knowing that history is good for me. It explains a few things. It gives me a tad more compassion in my heart.

Maybe you'll decide it's time to cut some slack to people who didn't help much in your younger days, but whom you realize now were doing as well as they could with the circumstances and the information they had.

The better able you are to do all that, the less likely you are to stew in a corrosive soup of regret and anger. The less likely you are to hold grudges and blame anyone else for your problems, the one thing that will surely keep you back as you're trying to get better.

Most important, you will inform yourself more about some things you probably should be handling a little differently right now. What I talk about in this chapter partly forms the research-based underpinning for many of the healthful self-regulation strategies that are at the core of this book.

All in the Family

Bipolar disorder does tend to run in families. The chemical imbalance in your brain, your sick brain, may have something to do with the genes you've inherited. The more family members you can point to with bipolar symptoms—parents, siblings, grandparents, aunts, and uncles—the more likely it was that you'd end up having it, too. Two-thirds of bipolars have at least one close relative with this illness or unipolar depression.

But a hard part of trying to map out a little family tree for yourself is that nobody used to talk about bipolar depression until recently, or even manic depression or even depression. It's only in hindsight now that maybe we decide, oh, *that's* what that was all about. The impressions we had at the time were all kind of shadowy and vague. Or we picked up the message that some things were just not to be talked about. That was the way a lot of us grew up.

A woman asked me, "How did you get your bipolar?" I
said, "I think when I was eleven a kid in school sneezed in
my corn." She looked at me and said, "Oh."

One woman remembered going to visit her grandparents
every other weekend as a child. "I adored my grandma, she was a
really jolly, kind of exuberant person, but then sometimes she
wouldn't join us. She stayed in her room. I'd be told she had 'a
little cold.' When we were getting ready to leave, my mom would
tell me to go say good-bye to Grandma. They lived in an apartment on the ground floor. Their bedroom was in the back, down a
long hall, and it faced the rear courtyard, so this was a dark place,
no natural light in there ever. To say good-bye to Grandma, I'd go
walk down that hall, open the door, and she was sitting in a chair
by the window, in the dark, staring out at the empty courtyard.
She never looked like she had a cold to me, but she also was different from the way I saw her at other times. This was always a little
spooky to me."

Another woman who wondered if bipolar disorder was what
was wrong with her uncle remembered "this sweet, jittery, nervous man who came to our family dinners and could not sit still.
I remember he would constantly run his hands through his hair.
And most often my mom wasn't sure if he'd show up at all, we
never knew if he'd be there. He lived alone, and for long stretches
of time we'd never hear from him at all and he wouldn't be
answering his phone. He took a two-week vacation every year and
drove, by himself, all the way from Massachusetts down to
Florida. When we saw him, he'd mention those trips, and I had

the feeling that was the only time he had some peace. He was very intelligent, but a strange man, with a lonesome air about him."

She also remembered references to her grandfather's brother, her great-uncle, "who had apparently spent some months in a state mental hospital. My grandfather got him out of there and the brother lived with them for a while, but went back in the hospital, and then died there when he was only about thirty-five or so. Just putting the pieces together from little dropped mentions here and there over the years, I figured out that my great-uncle committed suicide. But nobody in the family ever said it in so many words."

We put the pieces together.

My father—God love him!—was a fine man, a truly good person with a huge and generous heart. He went to work every day, never hit anyone, always helped out friends and neighbors in a hundred ways. He was also a functioning alcoholic, the Ricochet Rabbit in the house. That was a name my mother came up with. I'd be lying in bed at night, and I'd hear a bump . . . *damn* . . . scrape . . . *shit* . . . thump . . . *hell*. That was my dad coming home drunk, trying to get to his bed, and careening down the hall hitting the walls from one side to the other. My mom would say, "Here comes Ricochet Rabbit," and we'd laugh.

I guess it seemed funny. But there were lots of other nights when we weren't laughing. I remember now watching my mother cry, just sitting and crying in the darkened living room. I remember listening to her and my father argue about his drinking. Even today, memories of seeing my father passed out many evenings still bother me. Then one day this great guy, the father I loved and admired despite everything, decided to get better and stopped drinking. He was sober for the remaining seven years of his life. When he quit, he became active in AA, and he and I—I was in high school by then—went to a couple of schools and talked to the kids about alcohol abuse. I see now that he was a model for me, of how you can turn your life around, of how you can face your demons and help others face theirs.

My dad may not have been diagnosed, but it is crystal clear now, knowing what I do, that he was as bipolar as the day is long. Not all problem drinkers have bipolar disorder, of course, but a hefty amount of bipolars while they are sick and not getting treatment—about 50 percent, according to some estimates—do abuse alcohol at one time or other in an attempt to medicate themselves into some kind of stability. Cheer themselves up when depressed. Knock themselves out when their brains are racing and threatening to fly right out of their heads. Overeating is another way people who are battling manic or depressed feelings can try to make themselves feel better.

There can also be running through a family, and over generations, what researchers call "soft" signs of mood disturbances or mood sensitivity. These are behaviors or reactions that maybe never seem wildly extreme or drive people to get medical attention, but they're noticeable and recurrent. For example, a relative gets hit every year with SAD, seasonal affective disorder, or gloomy and depressed feelings during the winter. A relative—or maybe many of the women in a family—is highly moody and irritable for days before and after each menstrual cycle. Postpartum depression, some researchers suggest, also falls in this category.

And some "soft" signs might come across as personality traits: someone who's histrionic, always on the verge of hysteria over one thing or another; someone who tends to be paranoid; someone who's constantly anxious and worried about imagined illnesses.

Mapping Out a Genetic Predisposition

For a few good reasons it makes sense to take the time to draw up a little map of your family members in terms of their possible mood disorders. For one thing, as I've noted, knowing that you probably have a predisposition to bipolar disorder can relieve feelings of guilt or shame. For another thing, you will come up with elements of your history that might help a doctor correctly diagnose and treat you.

Your map—it can just be a page of notes—should include these family members: parents, grandparents, aunts, uncles, siblings. For each, write down any behaviors or circumstances that raise a red flag, remembering that the individuals involved may never have recognized or talked about "depression" or "manic depression" or "mood disorder." Following are some behaviors or circumstances that may mask the underlying illness:

- excessive use of alcohol
- binge eating and weight fluctuations
- unstable personal relationships over a long time
- suicide
- hospitalization for psychiatric reasons
- expression of gloomy or hopeless feelings
- reclusive behavior and "dropping out of sight" for long periods
- unpredictable angry outbursts on a regular basis

Put this family-related information in its proper place in your mind. Like I said, it might explain a few things and the family tree history can be a useful part of the "before" picture to share with the good doctor you find. But it shouldn't give any of us permission to play the blame game. You can't blame genetics; it is what it is.

Childhood Signs

I can trace my illness back to about the age of eleven. Maybe it was there earlier, but for some reason everything before that age is lost to my memory. I do see that I went through some mania back then when I was eleven and in the years following; mostly, however, I remember the sadness.

Young Paul was a boy who never quite fit in, not with the other kids in school and in the neighborhood. No real friends. All the cool kids—my two older brothers included—played sports, which I did not. Hell, I didn't even fit in with the "bad" boys and girls. I tried to hang out with a gang once, but that didn't take. Add to this picture the fact that I couldn't pronounce my *r*'s very well, and you had a kid who would do anything not to go to school as often as possible. The one thing I cared about was playing music, and I knew exactly what I was going to do when I grew up—write songs and be a rock and roll star, nothing more, nothing less.

Music was a big deal in our family, where just about every male played at least one instrument. At any family function, you could count on two happenings: first, at some point during the day or evening, music was being played, and second, there was major drinking. Drinking, smoking, playing music . . . yeah, that was what it was all about. And that turned out to be the way *my* life did seem to go for a long, long time.

It has been my joy and good fortune to have had so many very talented people to learn from over the years. The unfortunate truth, however, is that during my most impressionable times I only learned the bad stuff, and much of what would come to haunt me I picked up in and around the family. I spent many hours in bars with my father, uncles, and grandfathers, which are not good places for a young child and, in a lot of cases, not so great for an adult either. But that's where and how I had my first lessons in social behavior, and by age eleven or twelve I was smoking cigarettes and drinking, because I knew only what I saw around me— drink, smoke, play music. That was my way to be cool.

But mostly I remember the sadness. We kids had a lot of time alone. My parents both worked long hours, and I could pretend to be sick in order to avoid going to school and my mom would let me stay home because she was too busy to argue. The house would be empty and I could just hunker down in my closet. Yeah, I was a pioneer of being in a closet, sitting there on the floor and writing my little songs. This is when I started to wish that I was not alive. Not thinking of killing myself, but simply wishing not to be. Maybe I believed that if I wished hard enough it would happen, I would disappear.

So there I was in my closet, growing up without fitting in to much of anything, poisoning my already sick brain with the alcohol and the cigarettes, wanting not to be alive, and having no one to tell. I couldn't tell my mother because I didn't want to give her another thing to worry about—my father's drinking, one of my brothers getting into a lot of street fights, her need to work hard in order to keep us fed, and trying to keep us kids from falling too far off course in life were more than enough. But anyway, back then you just didn't tell your parents, or anyone else, about being sad. When I give one of my talks today, I sometimes say that if I'd told my mom I wanted to kill myself, she would have said something like, "Well, don't get any blood on my carpet." If I'd told my dad, his response would have been, "Don't use any of my tools." This gets a laugh, but it's actually close to the truth.

I never did act on my thoughts. I never did try to end my life. I never told anyone about the sadness. And I reached the so-called age of emancipation in so many ways incapable of leading a stable adult life.

Most researchers say that bipolar disorder typically begins in the teen or early adult years, though it can also start in childhood. "Official" statistics say that half of bipolar adults report having symptoms before they were seventeen, and in my opinion, that's a conservative estimate. Practically everyone I hear from at my talks remembers feeling or being "crazy," "different," "out of it" as a kid.

Maybe as a child you didn't get much understanding from the people around you. Maybe you got entirely the wrong kind of understanding. A man who is now in his early fifties said his parents "thought I was just a mean, aggressive punk. I was this kid who could not stop bouncing off walls. What they saw was disobedience, defiance. I got one punishment after another. None of this helped me." A woman, now forty-five, remembered herself as a fearful and anxious child. "I was scared of being left alone, scared of so many things. I had night terrors. I threw up a lot when I had to leave for school. When I was about eight or nine, I became obsessed with the thought that my mother was going to die, and I'd cry all the time. I think she was worried about me, but her attitude was to act kind of supercheerful and upbeat, I guess trying to have it rub off on me."

These are more enlightened times we live in, and there's better awareness of what can go wrong with kids and of the differences between "normal" growing pains and the pains of this illness. At the same time, the pendulum has maybe swung too far in the opposite direction, and everybody is quick to jump on the mental illness bandwagon and prescribe pills for everything unpleasant in the world. If grown-ups typically go through many years and several doctors before getting accurately diagnosed— and they do—the picture may be even worse for children and adolescents. The doc may come up with attention deficit disorder, attention deficit with hyperactivity, obsessive-compulsive disorder, depression, and a few other diagnoses—misprescribing medications along the way—before hitting on the right one.

If you are right now the parent of a youngster who's worrying you over behaviors and moods you can't figure out, I hope this book will inform you in a positive way as you go about finding help. If you are someone looking back at your own childhood in the wake of being diagnosed as bipolar, maybe you'll want to mourn a little for that mixed-up kid, admire how he or she nevertheless showed resilience and bravery in the face of confusion and rejection, and tell him or her *good job*. And then move on past the mourning.

The Hair-Trigger Effect

Evan, a man in his early thirties, told this story: "I would say that my symptoms started to appear when I went off to college, age seventeen, and for a few years after college, but it wasn't anything too scary. My first severe manic episode, which of course I didn't realize what it was at the time, happened when I landed an excellent job with an art auction gallery. I was really pumped about this for a few reasons, maybe mainly because I was showing up my parents. My parents had been vocally negative about my studying art history in college—I'd never get a job in the art field, never make any money, I should become a lawyer like every other male in my family. So this was vindication. My salary wasn't bad, plus I had a little income from a trust fund, so this was all enough for me to get my own place. From being a put-down kid to being a hotshot, self-supporting adult, overnight, that's what it felt like."

He signed up for half a dozen credit cards. He treated his parents, brother, and sisters to a fancy dinner his first week on the job. Over the six or seven months his mania went on, Evan went out every night and fell in with some new friends who partied a lot. "Most of the people I knew then were doing what I was doing. It didn't seem so bad. Buy a lot of stuff on credit, go out and have fun, burn the candle at both ends, you're young. But the guys I hung out with at night went back to their jobs in the morning and were okay. That's where I began to lose it completely." He started acting inappropriately with two young women in his office. "What was worse," Evan said, "I developed the fantasy that I was meant to take over the business. The owners were too unimaginative and passive, in my inflated opinion. I began trying to build up my own stable of people among the dealers and consigners we worked with, telling them I'd be opening my own gallery soon, they should stick with me, forget about these losers. Of course, this blew up in my face."

He was fired. He had to move back into his parents' house, fell into a depression, and struggled for a few years to get work and pay off his debts. He takes medication and is doing okay, but Evan believes that that one episode in his mid-twenties changed him, "maybe supercharged some of the synapses in my brain. I always went a little over the top with things, but it's like I'm on a hair trigger now. I have to be careful, because even small stuff can tend to start a mini cycle."

I don't know about supercharged synapses, but there is a lot of support from medical professionals for the hair-trigger possibility, or the idea that one major episode, prompted by something really good or really bad, can leave you more susceptible in the future to mood swings. Especially if you have a predisposition to bipolar disorder, based on your genes, on your childhood history, you can be more vulnerable after one of those major episodes, and it won't take a really big event—not a blowtorch, just a spark—to set you off. That should tell you about the need to keep aware of changes in routine, changes in sleep patterns, the "small stuff" that you have to regulate in some of the ways we talk about later in this book.

So, after these ideas about where bipolar disorder comes from, what starts it, who's to blame, now on to what to do about it.

FOUR

"Finally, It All Made Sense"

Reaching a Diagnosis

In a previous chapter, I wrote about my dark night of the soul, the culmination or the nadir of over three years of almost unrelieved depression. Stuck in the black hole. The best I experienced was an occasional period of lighter darkness; the rest of the time, my depression was having depression. I was pissing away friends the way you relieve yourself at a baseball game from all the beer you're drinking. My brothers and sister had basically vanished from my life. One or two associates knew I was depressed; most of the folks around me had no idea. It wasn't as if I could pick up the phone and tell my mother that I was mentally, emotionally, psychologically down-and-out. At this point, I wasn't Bipolar Boy yet, I was still plain old Paul Jones, and if plain old Paul Jones called his mom or anyone else, chances are he'd be told, Pull yourself together kid, it's all in your head!

One day, my D-day you could call it, I got a blessed second of sanity that would forever change my life.

I went to the doctor.

We who have bipolar disorder finally get help, I think, in one of three ways or because of one of three reasons: one, we're jailed and forced to do it; two, we act off-the-charts crazy or try to kill ourselves, get dragged into a hospital, and are forced to do it; and three, we seek help because we know the end is near. We just can't stand living anymore, it's too damn hard. That was me. I had been in the darkness for so long that I was running out of ways to escape it. In fact, I sort of suspected I was already dead and it was only a matter of time before they'd dispose of the body.

Why does it take getting tossed in jail, or landing on a psych ward, or being two steps away from shooting yourself to find something good, even just talking to people about our pain? Partly because nobody will pay attention. Remember my "acceptable depression chart"? That's why we are so reluctant to cry out. Nowhere on the chart does it allow time for being depressed for no obvious reason. Also, you go to a doctor when you're sick, and with this thing, you don't know if you're sick or what. It's not like saying you're having a little acid reflux problem. And then—and here's something I hear from so many bipolars I talk to—maybe you consulted one of these esteemed medical professionals, or more than one, and no way and no how did you get anything like the understanding, support, and appropriate advice that you so desperately needed. In fact, you may have been so emotionally bruised, disappointed, or embarrassed by the encounter that you swore off doctors for a long time after that. Various studies tell us that people spend on average *eight or more years* bouncing through four or more doctors before they learn they have bipolar disorder.

This chapter is about getting a correct diagnosis of your illness, starting with finding someone who'll give it to you. It's about the importance of connecting with the right doctor and avoiding a wrong one, because the right one will start you on the path to saving your life and a wrong one can keep you stranded. It's about what to expect when you get to the good doctor—what you will be asked or what you should plan to reveal—and how he or she is going to come up with the diagnosis of bipolar disorder. And we will talk about the before and after picture, what it feels like to get word finally on what's wrong with you—and those feelings can be surprising.

The Right Doctor: Where Is He or She?

Personally, I think the right doctor is one who is himself or herself bipolar, because that individual is going to know the score. Not so possible, obviously, so we must make do with the next best thing. That's someone with the proper credentials, of course, and someone who knows what he or she is talking about regarding mental illness. But the next best thing has also got to be a doctor you basically like as a human being, at least a little.

That's the ideal for any kind of medical problem, but factor in that you have a mental illness, and I think the need to have a doctor or doctors that you trust and like is magnified one hundred times. Because if you don't, you are not going to be upfront and honest, you will not feel safe enough to share your darkest secrets and fears, and you most certainly are not going to call him or her when you really should. You will hold off to the last minute to reach out for help and that, my friends, is how people die. In addition, there will be occasions when this person will have to work off instinct and the history of knowing who you are, because in all likelihood there will be times he or she will be seeing you when you are not entirely *you*. Your brain will be getting a little wacky again, and you'll maybe not be able to let the good doc know that because you don't realize it yourself. When you're controlling a mental illness, the doctor is going to be a continuing presence in your life for a long time. This is not a one-shot deal, in and out and you're on your way.

I have to say that I have been pretty lucky when it comes to encountering medical professionals. Even so, it has not been a bed of roses for me, and I'll give you an example on the next page. Finding the right doctor might be a long and winding road, but I think you can learn a little something from each one you meet, and strengthen yourself on the way. The worst action to take is no action at all, struggling along with someone who's not really getting the whole picture, or not understanding where you're coming from.

If you have a lousy doctor, change doctors. A bad doctor is a bad doctor, and there are plenty of the bad ones to go around—and by a bad doctor, I mean one who may have all the right medical qualifications, but with whom you feel uncomfortable and restricted. On the other hand, there are even more of the good ones. You just have to go out and find them.

You may argue, your insurance won't let you choose, the better doctors are all booked for months, and so on. That may be true; give it your best shot to get what you need, and then your best shot again if necessary. Taking an active role in your treatment is going to include working well with the physician who is doing the treating. If it comes to it, be honest and let the individual you've started seeing know that you're finding it difficult to strike up a positive relationship between the two of you, you're finding it hard to speak your piece and sense that you are being listened to, or whatever the problem is. The doctor might not like hearing this information, but at least you will start a conversation that may lead to a solution or to a referral to another physician.

Your lousy doctor may not like you either. So there.

> One doctor told me my mental illness was "all in your head." No joke. I wanted to say to that doc, "My foot is about to be all upside your rear."

I give this little preface because I've heard many horror stories from my fellow bipolar sufferers. At one of my talks, invariably someone will raise a hand or come up to me after and say it's just awful, it makes them nervous, it's unsatisfying to visit the doctor. One man said, "I think this guy I'm going to is pretty good, at least he's got a good reputation, but he's so arrogant, so above it all, I come out of there feeling about two feet tall. I also get the odd impression that he doesn't really take this seriously. He says some of the right words, but he doesn't really believe them, in a way." One woman said, "I've had several appointments with this person, and each time it's like I'm starting all over. It's like he doesn't seem to remember what we talked about the last time I was there. It starts when I call for an appointment, and the nurse or whatever she is asks me, 'And what should I tell the doctor you want to see him for?' Once there was another person on phone duty, and she asked me if I had ever seen the doctor before or was I new. It doesn't give me a lot of confidence. I think they should at least remember your name, you know?"

I agree.

They should remember our names. They should listen carefully. They should believe us and take us seriously.

Now, if you're not even that far yet—you're still at the point of thinking it's just getting too damn hard to go on living the way you're living, and you've got to go talk to somebody—where do you start? If you have a decent internist, family doctor, general practitioner, or primary care provider, start there. He might want to check out your overall health, make sure your thyroid or whatever is working as it should. He will probably refer you to a mental health professional, typically a psychiatrist, an M.D. who can write out prescriptions and is supposed to be an expert in the pharmacological control of mental illness—or better living through pills. You want to connect with one who specializes in mood disorders or has a lot of experience in that area. If you don't have a decent internist, family doctor, or so on, call the American Psychiatric Association and say you would like a recommended referral or two in your area.

As I say, it may be a long and winding road. But if you're persistent and/or you're lucky, you find the little light in the darkness. Which was my D-day.

The Good Doctor: Telling Your Story

My visit to my family doctor, Steve—the visit that changed my world—was really the first time I had ever admitted out loud to having an issue. I'd seen this man maybe once or twice a year to get some meds for a sore throat or something, and doctors' offices are my least favorite place to spend time. Now, in desperation, I made the appointment, showed up, and in walked Steve. He sat down, I sat down, we began to talk.

I'm not sure how long it took me to get the words out of my mouth. I'm not really sure what the words were, in fact. Steve did know this much about me: that I earned a living making people laugh, and that I had three great kids and a great wife, that I was a basic middle-class guy who seemed to have it all—everything that you're supposed to have at my age, the house, cars, motorcycle, wife, kids, dog, picket fence. But there I was, trying to explain that I wanted to die every single day and I had now begun dreaming about dying.

Steve asked me a lot of questions, we talked for what seemed forever—definitely longer than a normal visit. I remember crying at points, that's for sure. It's hard not to remember when you break down in front of a doctor. That was one of the toughest parts, yet also one of the best. I was talking about something I had hidden for over twenty-six years of my life—the sleeping in closets, under beds, waking up with chills, all that was being released on this day. As the words somehow managed to come out, I saw this man's face watching me not with pity or judgment, but with honest, caring emotion, and after a while, I felt as though I was with a friend who could and would listen to me. I can tell you now that Steve's reaction to my story will stay in my memory for all my days. Much of that visit is cloudy, to say the least. My mind was filled with illness and fuzz, and it had taken all I had to get to that office in the first place. But despite the illness and the fuzz, I knew I'd connected at last with a person who was going to help.

Finally, Steve looked at me and said, "Paul, I think that you're bipolar." What the hell was that? I immediately went on the defensive and told him that I was very happy with women and never would— He stopped me. "No, no, bipolar disorder, manic depression." Ah, manic depression, that I've heard of, that's something I can live with, right? Yes, Steve explained, it was something I could live with.

So it began, saving my life. Finally, something made sense.

I was lucky. But I think you can go in better prepared than I was, more organized, in a sense. If you are right now thinking about setting up this crucial appointment, you have the name of someone who has been recommended and sounds like one of the good ones, get things clear in your mind about what you should convey.

How does a doctor know you have bipolar disorder? How can he tell? These are interesting questions because, unlike most illnesses that may or may not hit us over the course of a life, there's no "concrete" evidence to nail the thing down. He can't tell by taking a blood sample or a little piece of your tissue somewhere and running some tests. He can't send you through a CAT scan machine. This may change in the future, because researchers are looking into some very sophisticated techniques, like taking images of the nerves in the brain and identifying what may be signs that some of those connections aren't functioning normally. Some medical scientists are examining hormone shifts in the body, and whether they are cause or consequence of bipolar episodes.

For now, however, the main way the doctor knows, or thinks he knows, is through listening carefully as you describe what's been going on in your life, and analyzing those symptoms. Which is why you must be frank, honest, thorough, and specific. A huge problem with this illness is that it can look and sound like a bunch of others—such as unipolar depression or anxiety disorder. And medications that might be good in treating those illnesses can be all wrong in the treatment of bipolar disorder.

Prepare yourself. Telling your story may be tough. Write down notes for yourself, if that seems like a good way to pull your thoughts together and remember what you want to say when you're in the doc's office. The kind of information that will help him reach a diagnosis, and a correct diagnosis, falls in three broad categories. He will ask you to explain what's been happening, how long it's been going on, and how bad it is.

What's been happening?

You want to talk about your depressed (down) moods and your manic (up) moods, but saying "I've been bummed out a lot" and "I've been pretty hyper" doesn't do it. Describe the feelings and

symptoms you have had or the behaviors that point to depression.
Those might include:

- everything around you seems empty and colorless

- you're finding no fun or pleasure in things you usually like

- you can't sleep or you're sleeping way too much

- you feel apathetic and sapped of energy

- you've been eating too much or not eating at all

- you've been getting too fat or too thin

- you believe you are no good to anybody and just generally a
  rotten person

- you blame yourself for all kinds of things that have gone
  wrong

- you can't focus on your work, can't concentrate

- you think about dying

Describe the feelings or symptoms when you're in an "up"
mood. They might include:

- you're having fifty thoughts at once

- you can't stop talking

- you believe you can do anything and everything

- you're spending money like crazy

- you're euphoric

- you hardly get any sleep but you don't need any

- you've got sex on your mind all the time

- you've been taking risky chances that actually could end up killing you or getting you arrested

- you think you're the one who can save the world

- you're irritable and cranky

- you've been feeling unusually anxious and panicky for no particular reason

Can you tie in any life events that occurred around the time your moods starting heading down or up? Someone you love just died or you won the lottery, you broke up with a boyfriend or you got a terrific new job. Negative or positive things that happen can trigger episodes. Or, on the contrary, maybe there's nothing specific to point to, and the moods don't seem to make sense.

How long has this been going on and how long does it last?

The doctor will want to know the time frames: You've been feeling this way every day for a month or for the last year. You get into a hyper, "up" mood that lasts for a couple of weeks, then just as quickly you get depressed. Maybe the moods are coming at you all at once, up and down in the course of twenty-four hours. Maybe you experience a period of three or four months when all is well, no symptoms, then you begin again to cycle up or down.

You don't have to go back to the dawn of time and describe ancient childhood miseries, though you can if you think it's relevant and certainly you should if you were suicidal, if you were or currently are on medications of any sort, or if you were treated by other medical professionals for mental problems. Also, if you have connected with one of the good docs, one who knows a thing or two about mental illnesses, he should ask you—or you should tell him—about any symptoms running in your family: your mom was always depressed, your dad was a serious drinker. A family history that points to mood disorders can help him diagnose what's probably your problem.

What this doctor most wants to understand, however, is the pattern of your mood swings in your life now.

How bad is it? Or, how seriously is it messing up the way you go about your day-to-day life?

A doctor will want to know what "normal" looks like for you, and how far you drift from normal when you're manic or depressed. Are your mood swings severe enough that you can't go to work, you pick fights with everybody, you don't get out of

The Bipolar Diagnosis

You know what being manic means and what depression means. If you are new to the whole experience of talking to medical professionals, you'll probably hear some of the following terms as well. These categories, put forth by the American Psychiatric Association and other organizations involved with mental illnesses, are often referred to and considered to be the official word on the several forms and aspects of bipolar disorder. Some researchers believe they give only a partially helpful framework for a diagnosis, and are hoping to further refine the picture in the years ahead.

Hypomania

Hypomania is an "up" mood with a lot of the characteristics of being manic, though not as potentially destructive and, typically, not including the loss of perspective that usually goes along with full-blown mania. During a hypomanic period, which can feel attractive and exciting—to you and to others watching—you have a lot of energy, you're confident, stuff is getting done, you're maybe impatient and a little irritable. You're still functioning in the world pretty well.

Bipolar disorder I

Being diagnosed with bipolar I means you have experienced at least one major manic or mixed episode, and possibly one or more depressed episodes as well.

Bipolar disorder II

This is described as having at least one major depressive episode and at least one hypomanic episode.

The explanations of hypomania, bipolar I, and bipolar II include time frames (such as, the episode lasted for at least one week or for a two-week period) and number of symptoms (such as, three

continues on next page . . .

continued from previous page . . .

or more or five or more of the symptoms associated with mania and with depression—racing thoughts, lack of sleep, apathy, difficulty concentrating, and so on).

Mixed state

In mixed bipolar disorder, you experience serious "up" manic moods and serious "down" depressive moods at the same time, or both happening nearly every day for a week or more. This is considered the most explosive situation, when suicidal behaviors or thoughts or paranoia can enter the picture.

Rapid cycling

You have four or more episodes of manic, hypomanic, or depressive moods within one year.

Cyclothemia

This is a kinder, gentler form of mood cycling. You have hypomanic and depressive episodes, but not the full-blown versions of either.

These distinctions have meaning and importance to your doctor, because they have a lot to suggest about treatment, the medications and therapies you should receive. Myself, I have not and do not put a great deal of thought into the whole classification matter. To me, the important thing is not *what* you're diagnosed with exactly, but what you *do* with your diagnosis. Or I'll put it this way: it's not so much what type of bipolar illness a person has, but what type of person has it. I've met individuals who say they are bipolar II, the not-so-bad version, who cannot seem to function at all. I've also met people who supposedly have the worst of the worst aspects, and they're out there fighting every single day and living life successfully and fully.

bed for days? Have they landed you in the hospital? If you're functioning kind of okay, you're doing what you have to get done, that tells him one thing. If you are crashing and burning, that's another thing.

That's the gist of it, the pieces of your story that the good doctor will put together to decide what's wrong with you and what you need in order to fix it.

The Not-So-Good Doctor: Be Prepared

Now, another story from my journeys into doctorland, and a type of experience that, unfortunately, you are likely to run into at some stage on your own journey. There is a tremendous, added strain from needing to speak to a new, strange doctor and spill out your unhappy, complex tale yet again—and worse than a strain if you come up against an unfeeling, not-getting-it brick wall of one kind or another.

Dr. Steve had been open and honest with me concerning my treatment. He made it clear that he was not well versed in the illness he had diagnosed me with, and strongly suggested I see a psychiatrist. To which I said, "No way!" However, a couple of months into this new diagnosed life of mine, I realized maybe Steve was right. I was taking the medications he had prescribed, but things were not better. Still living in darkness, still entertaining harsh thoughts of suicide, I got a referral for what would be my first visit to a head doctor, as I lovingly call them. That's what they specialize in, your head.

I am not sure if you have ever had to call a doctor of psychiatry for an appointment, but let me tell you this: it hurts your head even more than it hurts already. No wonder people end up dead. It's tough just to get in the door, like a very exclusive country club. If they find out you're paying by cash or check, you might as well have the black plague.

Anyway, there I was, walking into a huge clinic-type place. I went up to the front desk, announced myself, got a short "Hello, Mr. Jones" from the receptionist, and the next words out of her mouth were, "Will you be writing a check or will it be cash?" I told her I'd be writing a check. Her words after that were: "You should know there is a twenty-five-dollar fee on a returned check." This comment just about sent me into a Bipolar Moment. There I was, very, very sick—and, as it happened, with more money in my checking account at the time than that lady probably made in a year—and she was already treating me like crap.

That's how people with mental illnesses are treated every day. I was a sick individual, and the receptionist's concern was my $125, with the assumption that my piece of signed paper was probably going to bounce. Well, I wrote my check, sat down in the waiting area, heard my name called, and went back to see the doctor. Here is the visit the way it happened. I remember this day as if it were yesterday. It contributed to my overall wariness of the medical field as it is involved in mental illness, and it is one reason I have wanted to write in this book about the good doctors and the bad doctors, the right ones and the wrong ones.

The doctor introduced herself with little feeling, not looking at me, and then proceeded to a cross-examination: Who had recommended her? How long had I known that person? Was I married? How long? How many kids? How old? Mother alive? Father alive? This is how our conversation continued:

DR. HEAD: What's going on with you?

ME: Well, I've been told I am bipolar. I just want to—

DOCTOR: Who told you that?

ME: My doctor.

DOCTOR: Is he a psychiatrist?

ME: No, he's my family doctor.

DOCTOR: How does he know you're bipolar?

ME: Well, I don't know *how* he knows, that's just what he suggested.

DOCTOR: How was your relationship with your father?

ME: Uh, it was fine.

DOCTOR: Were you abused?

ME: Excuse me? What do you mean?

DOCTOR: Did your parents abuse you?

ME: Excuse me again, but why would you ask that?

DOCTOR: Are you going to let me do my job?

(Now this is where the old Paul Jones started to kick in.)

ME: Are you shitting me? Ma'am, I want to ask a question. Is bipolar illness a chemical imbalance in the brain?

DOCTOR: Yes.

ME: Then what does all this you're talking about have to do with getting my brain fixed? My brain is sick and—

DOCTOR: Are you going to let me do my job?

ME: Excuse me?

DOCTOR: I said, are you going to let me do my job?

ME: Ma'am, I'm a thirty-seven-year-old man who wants to die every day, can we fix that?

DOCTOR: I'm going to prescribe you with [here she mentioned a particular medication].

ME: I'd prefer not to take that, if you don't mind, because of some of the side effects.

DOCTOR: Like what?

ME: Well, for one thing, I really don't have time to have my blood checked on a regular basis—

DOCTOR: Why not?

ME: Because I'm on the road a lot. Look, I've been doing a little research into this stuff, and I see there are other pills we can start off with that would not require the blood test, so I'm wondering if—

DOCTOR: Are you a doctor?

ME: No.

DOCTOR: Then please let me do my job.

ME: But I do not want to take those particular pills.

DOCTOR: I would prescribe this to my own children.

(More of the old Paul Jones, kicking it up a notch.)

ME: Then, you know what? You go ahead and prescribe them to your little lab monkeys, but I do not want to take that medication.

DOCTOR: If you are not going to let me do my job, you can leave.

ME: See ya.

I walked out of her office, told the lady at the front desk to enjoy my $125, got back in my car, and headed down the highway.

Why do I describe this little exchange to you? It goes back to the good, the bad, and the ugly in doctorland. I was desperate, but this so-called professional was more interested in a list of questions that really didn't have much to do with getting to know about my life that day. Worse: she seemed unable to see or hear what I was saying; my protests were dismissed as unimportant; she assumed a position of superior knowledge because she was a doctor and I was not a doctor. And more: where was the humanity in her words and her tone? Doctors are instructed, First, do no harm. She did me harm that day—by treating me as somewhat less than a reasonably intelligent adult and by making me wonder if I was ever going to get some real help.

On the way to getting properly diagnosed, and along the journey that follows—when you may need to see a specialist or you move and you've got to find a new doctor or whatever—you may run into one of the ugly ones. They are not bad in the sense of medical ignorance or lack of official qualifications. The head doctor who didn't want to hear what I was saying probably started out hoping to help people. Somewhere along the line, maybe, she lost sight of that and it all became about money. Or it became about playing God in people's lives, and nobody is allowed to question or go to bat with God.

Don't lose heart. Do not allow yourself to be diminished or belittled. We bipolars do inform ourselves along the way, we will pick up information about different treatments and about how our bodies react, and we are right to ask questions or challenge assumptions and expect to be listened to.

What Your Doctor Should Tell You, but Maybe Won't

I am going to put words in the doctor's mouth. If this is your first meeting or early on in your association with this medical professional, you should hear some version of the following. Too many people are not told the truth by their doctors or by others who are treating them. Some doctors may not themselves be fully *aware* of the truth. Some may consider that giving out a prescription concludes their role; what happens after that, well, just swallow the bitter pill, struggle through, you'll feel better eventually. And I think maybe a few might be motivated by misguided kindness ("I don't want to give this poor guy the bad news, because he'll get discouraged, and I know if he just does what I tell him he'll improve").

Getting accurately diagnosed is a blessing. But a good doctor should also convey the bad news, because there is some you need to hear if you're going to stay actively involved with your recovery, including:

- "This is a hard illness to live with."
- "There is no cure."
- "Medication can help control it, but it will take time, maybe a lot of time, to find the right combination of pills."
- "You may experience side effects that are not pleasant."
- "You may feel even worse before you start feeling better."
- "The medication regimen you begin with may work well for a while, and then not so well, and we'll have to try something else."
- "Keep in touch with me."

If you're not hearing any of this, turn the above statements into questions and ask them of your doctor.

"Here's What's Wrong with You": On Getting the News

On the day I was informed by Dr. Steve that bipolar disorder was a new word for manic depression, I had a ton of questions. He did not have all the answers and told me so. But going through my mind was: *Thank God! Now I know it's not my wife, kids, mother, father, house, girlfriend, dog, cat, or anything else. I know it's not all in my head—or actually it is, but in a different and better way. I'm not just a rotten, lousy person, I'm not imagining there's something wrong with me, now I know there is, but there's actually a name for this craziness and there's something that can be done about it.*

The weight of the world dropped from my shoulders. A million pounds lifted from my back. I cannot remember ever having anything feel so physically refreshing, so fantastically good, as that moment. At the time, I believed my nightmare was coming to an end. Steve had just offered me parole of sorts, an explanation for a darkness that hurts more than any other pain.

I walked out of his office with my new bottle of pills, and to my car with a little extra kick in my step, possibly a smile on my face. Yes! I am bipolar! Phew, what a relief, I have a mental illness, I'm the luckiest guy in the . . . whoa . . . whoa . . . whoa.

As I opened the door to my 1994 Corvette and got in, it hit me. *I have a mental illness.* How do I tell my wife, my children, my mother, my friends, all the people who are close to me? How do I tell myself? The car door slammed, and I distinctly remember that slam scaring me to death. It sounded like the prison door shutting in one of those movies where you watch the prisoner walk into his stone-cold cell, the camera shows the door closing, the bang of the door echoes, the prisoner's head turns, he looks out in despair. He's staring at the reality that he is in jail. Maybe forever.

My eyes went up to the rearview mirror, and I saw I was crying, and I mean, crying my eyes out. Do you remember being a kid and something bad happened, and you cried so hard that you could not breathe? That was me. People were walking by my car looking at me like I was a crackpot, and I honestly could not stop crying.

It's tempting—and natural—to think that once somebody names your disease, once somebody finally hits the nail on the head and gives you a recognizable explanation for all the stuff that's been going on with you for years, once somebody listens and hears and seems to know what he's talking about, well, then the floodgates of relief open. Now you know.

The floodgates of relief do open—for some of us, not all, and below I share with you some very different, but very common reactions. But relief is just the beginning, and maybe short-lived. A friend of mine was diagnosed with cancer, and he said this: "It's funny, I used to wonder what it's like to know you have cancer. Now I know. This sounds weird, but it's almost like I don't have to worry about getting cancer, because I got it. It's almost like the other shoe dropped. And you move into another kind of world, the world of people who have cancer." I found his observation interesting. We who learn we have bipolar disorder move into mental illness world, and, maybe unlike in cancer world, there's little sympathy or understanding.

Had anyone knocked on my car window that afternoon and asked if I was okay, and had I replied, "I just found out I'm mentally ill," that person would have scurried away in a hurry. That's another awful thing about this disease. We go running *toward* people with cancer, we try to say comforting words, ask if there is anything we can do to help, make casseroles for their families to be supportive in their time of trouble. Announce that you're mentally ill, and you're lucky you don't get a few phone calls from people asking you to stay away from their house and their kids.

I'm exaggerating, of course, but after diagnosis, the stigma settles in fast. And the first stigma reaction I had to deal with was mine. I was crying out of fear, worry, maybe, but mostly out of self-pity. Poor, poor me. Anyway, that was a cry I had coming to me. I needed that one, and let me tell you, I rode it for all I could. Then I realized it was time to stop, and I did.

The Hard Part Coming Up

Learning that you have a chemical imbalance in your brain and you can do something about it, this is good. But it comes as a nasty surprise to a lot of newly diagnosed bipolars that improvement is going to be a long time in coming. For me, it was about a year and a half before we, Dr. Steve and I, finally got it right. Is my story typical? Unfortunately, the answer is yes.

Part of the challenge will be trying to find the right combination of medications among the many variations used to treat bipolar disorder. Part of the challenge will be considering a raft of

Reacting to the News: A Wild and Crazy Range of Possible Emotions

You can experience any one feeling or several feelings that may surprise and distress you. It's normal. Your understanding of yourself has shifted in a major way. Relief, anger, anxiety, jubilation, fear, that all could be part of the picture. According to some research, people on average require about *seven years* to fully accept their condition, with often much vascillating in between. Be prepared.

Following are some reactions I have heard expressed by various people upon receiving the diagnosis of bipolar disorder.

> *"All the good, creative stuff I've done in my life—and there has been good, creative stuff—was just because I was sick."*

This man looked back on years of productivity as an investigative journalist and felt his accomplishments had to be chalked up to his mental health, or actually his lack of it. The accomplishments seemed suspect, like all the good creative stuff somehow didn't count now. But this is the "I am my sickness" perspective. Not everything, neither the good nor the bad, is fueled by your bipolar disorder. You are not your sickness.

> *"This can't be right. My family is the sanest, healthiest, feet-on-the-ground group of characters you're likely to meet."*

No, no, no, it's all a mistake. People come up with any number of reasons to deny or outright reject their bipolar diagnosis. If that's you, get a second opinion and a third opinion. Bipolar disorder does tend to run in families, but it doesn't have to be in your family for you to have it.

> *"This is embarrassing, shameful. How do I tell people?"*

I would hope that over time you get past feelings of shame and embarrassment. In any case, maybe you don't have to tell people.

Not everybody, at least, or not right now. In chapter 8, on educating others, are some thoughts on how to share the news and with whom.

> *"I'm wondering if I'll be able to do any of the things I've thought about, or if I have to alter my life goals."*

A woman at one of my talks said her immediate reaction was to begin mentally rescheduling her whole life, and as she described it, this really was *her whole life:* no more going to parties (too stimulating), scrap the idea of applying to law school (too stressful), forget the planned three-week vacation in Europe with her sister (different time zones, very threatening), and so on. From my own experience, it's probably smart not to make major life changes during the initial stages of treatment, but you do *not* have to assume that everything you hoped for and dreamed of is now in the toilet. Allow yourself a little time living in mental illness world, and see what kinds of activities you might want to adjust or let go of and what others you can handle just fine.

> *"I kind of freaked out. You hear the news, and there's this little feeling that you wish you hadn't asked. It's almost like, the devil you know is worse than the devil you don't know."*

It's better to know, it really is. And most of us get over the freak-out stage.

> *"If only I had learned about this years ago, everything would have turned out differently, everything would have been so much better."*

That may be true. And it's a sad thought. I personally will always regret that I did not get help sooner, but you have to try not to let the regret eat away at you. I heard a guy on TV, I think he was a pro football player, pooh-poohing some recent losing games he'd been in with the explanation, "That's not important anymore, it's all about the now." Yeah! There you go! It's all about the now.

other factors that have to do with lifestyle and habits and attitude, and that will play a role in how your medications work. What do you eat? How often do you eat? Do you take drugs? Get enough sleep? Are you a drinker? Do you smoke? What other pills are you taking? Throw in the fact that you are probably depressed, maybe in some form of trouble, maybe broke, and maybe you've alienated everyone you know, and you have one big battle ahead of you. Hell, most non-mentally ill people are less than successful at changing bad habits and lifestyles toward healthier patterns.

The one thing you must really try to understand about this illness we share is that it is truly an individual illness. Through all my traveling and speaking to groups, I have yet to run into any two people who are being treated in an identical manner and having identical success along an identical time line.

In the following two chapters—about medication and lifestyle matters—I want to talk about those issues in detail. Here, I want to say that it's hard because you must participate, you must get in the game or the fight, a kind of boxing match between you and your illness. But it can be done. It is being done every day by millions of people, though we don't hear about it or see it in the spotlight because many of us in the struggle are not willing to share our issues surrounding mental health in general. I am doing it. I'm happy to say that I'm living a good life as a person with a mental illness, living a life in a positive, productive manner. So fight the fight.

One more thought, and this is a big one: Being diagnosed with bipolar disorder gives you the reason you have been feeling the way you have been feeling for years. It does not give you an excuse for the things you have done. For me, I will never say that I drank myself silly, that I had affairs with women because I was sick with bipolar disorder. I did all that drinking, I had those affairs because I was a grown man who could not understand why he could not be happy, why he was depressed all the damn time. The drinking, the affairs, that was me searching for something I was never going to find. Once I was diagnosed, I had the reason for my depressions and the solution for them.

Don't look for excuses.

FIVE

"I Have to Say, the Meds Saved Me"

Prescription Medications and Their Benefits, and Staying Medicated

During the bad old days, half the time I was thinking, "I'm going to kill myself," and the other half, "I'm just a little stressed out, nothing buying a new car won't fix, who needs pills, I can handle this myself."

Wrong. I could not handle this myself. I did need pills, and I can say that prescription medication literally gave me my life back.

Why do you need medication? You are aware that you can never be pronounced "cured" of bipolar disorder and, in addition, that at some future point you may have a recurrence; the symptoms that went away or eased will return. Get on a good medication regimen, take the pills, and a relapse of major proportions is significantly less likely. You may still have manic-depressive episodes, but the ups don't go so up and the downs don't go so down, and they don't last as long as before. Take the pills and, according to some researchers who have been following these things, you have a one in three chance of staying *completely free* of symptoms forevermore. Those odds are not great, but they're not bad, either.

Take the pills, and you should stop thinking about killing yourself. I am living proof. After all those years of "suicidal ideation," as they call it, now that I've found the meds that work for my illness, I never consider *not* living, even when I'm off my beat, falling into a bit of a funk, and feeling pissed at the world.

Starting on a regimen of medication is almost always necessary. But many who have been down that road wish in retrospect that they had asked more questions and heard more answers. "Gird yourself with as much information at the start," says one, "so you understand what you can expect." I hope to gird you here with a little of that news.

The first thing I want to say about medications, however, is that I will not name names. As I put it on my website, I'm not a doctor and have never played one on TV. I will not mention any drugs that I am on now or that I have ever taken over the years. The reason is simple: I don't want to sway anyone about a treatment program. No two people are the same and no two treatments are the same. What has been successful for Bipolar Paul may not be what you need. And, of course, this is a tricky business that requires expert medical advice, tracking over time, and, quite often, mid-course adjustments along the way.

A Few Frequently Asked Questions, and a Few Short Answers

If you are well on your way to figuring out how to live with bipolar disorder and getting better—that is, you have been to a good doctor, you have been accurately diagnosed, you've begun treatment—you probably know all this already. If you are not there yet, or if you, my reader, are the relative of a loved one whom you hope to persuade that it's time to get medical advice, this brief overview may be useful background, a good starting place.

How does this stuff work?

Whatever drug (or combination of drugs) you are prescribed, it works to bring you down from an acute manic episode or up from an acute depression, and then to keep you on a relatively even keel after the acute stage is over. Exactly *how* it does that, I don't know. Nobody knows exactly, in fact, except that the medication does something good to your neurotransmitters and improves your brain chemistry.

Why do I have to take more than one med?

Different medications are intended to do different things, or to combat various bipolar symptoms. Some people do okay on just one type of pill, but most need a combination.

Are side effects inevitable and unavoidable?

Inevitable, probably. Supposedly some individuals experience no side effects whatsoever, but I've personally never run into any of those folks. Unavoidable, not necessarily. Your doctor may adjust the dosage, recommend simple steps you can take to reduce unpleasant effects (like taking your pills after a meal so you don't get sick to your stomach), or add another medication that will

continues on next page . . .

continued from previous page . . .

counter the side effect (like a sedative if you can't sleep). In the box on page 89, I list some of the typical side effects people experience.

How is the dosage decided?

If you are in an acute phase, very manic or very depressed, you'll probably get zapped with a high dosage. If you're fairly stable, or in the maintenance phase after an acute episode, there's a bit of a hit-or-miss aspect to getting the right amounts. A doctor might start you out slow and increase the dosage over time, watching out to see how it's working and what side effects are occurring.

What are the blood tests for?

Depending on what you're taking, you may have to have blood drawn from time to time. Blood tests reveal the levels of drugs in your system, and the goal is to have just enough in there to get good results, but no more. Blood tests also keep tabs on how other parts of your body besides your brain are holding up, because certain meds can mess around with your liver, your kidneys, your pancreas, your thyroid gland, and other things.

The tests might be necessary once a week at the start, then every month or at other intervals, or when you're reporting in on a semi-emergency basis because of a recurrence of symptoms or concerns that you're starting to cycle. Blood tests are a nuisance and a pain, just another not-fun aspect of bipolar disorder you have to deal with.

Do any of the so-called natural products on the market work?

I don't have personal experience with these supplements, but there is good research showing that omega-3 fatty acids are important in controlling both mania and depression.

Take the time and make the effort to understand just how the pills are designed to work and what you may experience once you start on them. Don't take the time or make the effort, and you're in mortal danger of continuing to live in a dark hole. I firmly believe that this is a major factor separating those of us who will survive from those who will remain sick, who will never get better.

Finding the Mix: Getting Started

Real improvements have been made in the use of medications to treat our disorder, and some previous miscalculations have been corrected. For example, lots of people went to doctors for years with complaints of feeling down, sad, miserable, and were sent away with a prescription for an antidepressant ("I've been on every antidepressant ever discovered in the universe," said a friend of mine). Big mistake. Antidepressants may do the job in a case of unipolar depression, but often have a disastrous effect on bipolar disorder. Doctors now know that when used alone those drugs can kick off a really bad manic episode. They overcorrect for the depression. So these days antidepressants are given in combination with other pills.

When you enter the wonderful world of medications, you'll hear some unsettling or scary words, like anticonvulsants and antipsychotics. Calm down. Just arm yourself with a general idea of what the different drugs are and why they should be good for you. Typically, they fall into three categories or types: mood stabilizers, antidepressants, and antipsychotics.

Mood Stabilizers

These are used to get you over an acute episode, either manic or depressive, or to stop new episodes from occurring. The two most commonly prescribed ones are lithium and divalproex, which most people know by the brand name Depakote.

Lithium is considered to work very well for bipolars who experience "pure" manic episodes, or terrific highs and euphoria not mixed in with simultaneous depression. The "up" mood may be followed with a "down" mood, but it's not all happening at the same time, and there's no rapid cycling. It's also good for people with a bipolar family history. Some respond well to lithium alone; some don't, and they can enjoy better results with a mix.

Depakote is an anticonvulsant, used for many years as a treatment for seizures in the control of epilepsy. Fortunately for us bipolars, it apparently is also effective with the kind of brain illness we have. This medication is considered good for people who have mixed episodes (depression and mania together), who are rapid cyclers, or who also have substance abuse problems or anxiety disorders.

Antidepressants

As the name says, these pills are used to treat the symptoms of depression. Typically, they build up slowly and take a while to work. There are lots of them on the market, with brand names like Wellbutrin, Prozac, Paxil, Zoloft, and Effexor. Always, as mentioned, you're going to be prescribed a mood stabilizer along with an antidepressant.

Antipsychotics

These may be used at a time of a major episode of depression or mania when the bipolar is hallucinating or delusional. Some doctors also say antipsychotics can work to stabilize moods and as sedatives, so they may be offered in combination with standard mood stabilizers even when the bipolar isn't having any psychotic symptoms. Newer antipsychotic medications, called atypicals— among them, brand names Clozaril, Risperdal, and Abilify—have fewer side effect risks than did the older generation and are the ones most commonly used.

This is a very broad overview of what medicating is all about. It's a complicated business. There are dozens, maybe hundreds of other brand names besides the ones I've mentioned above. I'm all in favor of doing some sleuthing and research on your own into the different meds. Check them out online. Listed in the resources section at the end of this book are some useful sites with good information. Consider the benefits and the requirements for taking a particular kind of pill, and talk it over with your doctor. For example, regular blood tests are a problem for me and many others. One, I'm terrified of needles. If I could walk into a doctor's office, have him punch me in the nose, and give my blood sample that way, then maybe okay. But needles, no. Second, I'm on the road all the time and can't get in for a test every thirty days. So we factored that into the equation of what particular meds were best suited to my illness, my little phobias, and my lifestyle.

Keep in touch with your doc. Nobody *loves* going to the doctor. When he says, "Come back in three months," you let out a *whew*, you've got a reprieve for a while. But before you're stabilized on a medication regimen, it's the better part of wisdom to check in, maybe with a weekly or even daily phone call, to discuss how it's going, your symptoms, side effects.

Most of us don't like to "bother" the doctor. If he's a good one, if he's insisted you keep in touch with him, it's not a bother. Definitely call right away—don't wait for your next appointment—if you are harboring suicidal feelings; if you are experiencing big changes in sleeping or other regular life patterns; or if you're being scheduled for surgery, a root canal, or any major assault on your body that will require you to be under anesthesia, take antibiotics, or add other chemical complications to what you're doing already.

After Day One: What You Can (and Can't) Expect

In one election in recent memory, a politician running for state office campaigned with the rousing slogan, "On day one, everything changes." That cheery, optimistic, gung-ho promise was his way of telling voters that once he was elected, all the accumulated woes and disappointments and failings of recent years—accumulated by the the miserable, low-life politicians he was planning to replace—would disappear, virtually overnight. Everything changes.

That's what many of us with bipolar disorder tell ourselves. So many people I speak with seem to think that getting a prescription is the end of their troubles. So many people are then broken in spirit and determination, because they believed they were supposed to wake up the next morning or at least a week later feeling infinitely much better. When it doesn't happen, suddenly they are down further than they were before; or worse, they begin to doubt what their doctor said.

It's not difficult to understand why that upbeat mindset is so attractive. Merilee, a woman in her early thirties, explained it beautifully:

"You're going along for years not really knowing what your problem is, much less what you need to do to get over it. Maybe you've gone to a couple of doctors, and one gave you an antidepressant and that didn't work very well for very long. The other one decided you needed to see a psychologist and get some therapy, because you needed to change your quote-unquote 'negative thinking.' That was my experience, in fact.

"Maybe at points in those years you tried to diagnose yourself: okay, I'm drinking way too much wine, I'll stop that, and I'm not getting enough sleep, I can fix that. So you do those things, you feel a little better briefly, you figure maybe the whole thing has gone away, whatever the 'thing' is. Before long, you're back cycling again.

"Then, wonder of wonders, you connect with a doc who spends a good deal of time with you, who listens carefully to what you're describing, who asks a lot of questions, who says you almost surely are bipolar, and who tells you there are extremely effective medications to deal with that.

"Bingo! At last, somebody's figured you out and knows what you need and is going to help. You eat this up. Your new life is going to start, like, tomorrow, as soon as you can get to the drugstore with those little pieces of paper with the names of the magic pills on them. It's predictable. We live in a society that promotes the medicalization of all our ills. Somebody in a position of authority puts a label on what you have, and you feel in your bones that it's right, at last somebody gets it. And the second part is, we have such faith in the power of pharmacology to cure what ails us. So yes, just let me get my hands on those pills, and all will be well."

Rarely is all well just like that, as Merilee and so many others of us have discovered. It's a journey you are on.

For me, the medication journey took about a year and a half. The one thing I can say is that when, after some weeks of starting treatment, I wasn't any better, it came as no great surprise. As I've mentioned, my fine doctor, Steve, made it quite clear that it might well take a long time before I was feeling 100 percent, if there even was such a thing. But that was a hard year and a half, because not only was I still sick, not only had I found no real relief from my symptoms, I was also dealing with a lot of questions and adjustments. Swallowing pills, not feeling any better, and now experiencing unpleasant stuff that I hadn't run into before, like being fat and tired and sexually limp—or at least, I hadn't run into them all at the same time.

Let me share with you two stories, some of my own early responses to treatment. The first story is pretty serious; the second one, not so serious. I share them not to scare you, but to shed some light on what can happen—and so that it maybe won't come as a shock to you when you discover you're on a bumpy road.

One day I was sitting in a chair staring at the pictures of my children on top of my computer monitor. I wanted to die; I never slept without dreaming about blowing my head off. I was out of direction and out of my mind to the point of no return. And this was about *six or eight months into treatment*! I was taking the medication, I was doing what I was supposed to do, I was getting help. It wasn't working.

On that day, I decided to commit suicide. This was something different from the "maybe I'll just drive a hundred miles an hour and accidentally go off a cliff and that will take care of that" behaviors that I've described earlier, living so that my life would be taken from me out of stupidity. This was a conscious, considered decision.

Once my mind was made up, I thought the whole thing through, how it would work. My first idea was to blow my head off—a really cool guy approach. Dramatic, manly, leaving splatters, leaving a really cool mess. But I did have a little reality check: I'm not an especially lucky person and I figured there was a good chance I'd botch it. I'd end up paralyzed in a chair with tubes in my nose and unable to speak, and have to watch my wife date other men who would get to ride my motorcycle and be friends with my kids. So I scratched the gun scenario. My second idea was hanging myself—also manly and at least *kind of* a mess. Plus, I was planning to get creative on where to do it. But I happened to watch the old Clint Eastwood movie *Hang 'Em High*, in which some guys try but fail to hang Clint, who goes through the rest of life with a scar across his neck. That would be my luck, too, I thought, and it would irritate me no end to walk around with people saying, "Eeewww, Paul, what happened to your neck?" and having to tell the whole story.

So I decided to attach myself to my more feminine side and take pills, which I probably couldn't screw up. At my local Walgreen's the next morning, I bought enough sleeping pills to pretty much kill a horse, and I kissed my family good-bye. I can talk lightly about all this now, but on that day there was not a doubt in my mind that my life would be over within the next ten or so hours. I was done.

Not yet, obviously, as it turned out. I mentioned in the introduction my eight-hour session writing out a suicide letter, by the end of which I'd decided maybe I would stick around a little longer. A couple of weeks after that, a longtime friend happened to call me and asked how I was doing, and for some reason, I sent him my letter. He read it and called me back. "Paul, I'm not depressed," he said, "I'm not suicidal, but you just changed my life with what you wrote. You should talk about this stuff. You can help a lot of people." That made the world look a little brighter. I got back to my good doctor and got another med to help me through the dark spell.

Now the second story.

So many of the tales about my bipolar life in this book revolve around hotel rooms and my car, because hotels and cars are where I spent the bulk of my time during those years, and this story will be no different.

I was packing my bags to head home from a gig in Detroit. It was about 6:30 a.m., and I had been taking my meds for about four months with no effect—but my wife kept reminding me that it was only a matter of time before we hit on the right mix, and that was enough to keep hope alive for yet another round of adjustments. On this morning, I was tired, down, throwing stuff in my suitcase, standing there just in my underwear (a visual most of you do not wish to dwell on, I am sure). Reaching for my shampoo on the bathroom counter, my eyes went to the mirror and what did I see? A fat, bloated guy I'd never met before in my life. Now, I am here to tell you that I was scared out of my mind. Who was this slob standing in my room, big old belly hanging over his Fruit of the Looms, eyes puffy with bags underneath sagging in the same manner as the belly?

Confession: I am not now, nor have I ever been, a truly fine specimen of a man, but one thing I have never been was this fellow I was looking at. Staring at the new Fat Paul, to go along with Bipolar Paul, I began to get angry, hurt, and, especially, depressed. A few months ago I learned I was mentally ill; bad enough that I had a screwed-up brain, now my body had turned into flab.

My reaction: *Paul, you're a fat-ass, stupid jerk. You can't even button your pants anymore. Who would want to hire you? No one, that's who. Why are you letting them do this to you? You need to have your head examined, is what you need. Stop taking the pills and learn to live with being bipolar. What are you, some kind of sissy? Cut it out, get to a gym, get yourself back in shape. Screw this crap! If this is what you have to look like in order to not be crazy, then to hell with it.*

So I grabbed the bottles of pills off the table, threw them in the garbage. Got in my car and headed for home, still cussing myself. Then I came to a stop sign, and I remember now placing both hands on the steering wheel and resting my head. I took a deep breath, pulled a U-turn, and drove back to the hotel. Got the key back to my former room and got the pill bottles out of the trash. As I came back up, I looked in the mirror again, only this time I saw my wife's face looking back at me. And I could hear her say, clear as a bell, "It's only a matter of time, Paul."

I have never missed a pill since then, and I never will. (I did something about Fat Paul, too: ate less, ate better, exercised more. Big mystery.) Sticking with it, working with my good doctor, I eventually hit on a medication combination that worked. And I know that if this current mix stops working, it will again be just a matter of time until we find the new right one.

The lesson here is: in the beginning, and the beginning may go on for months, you might feel worse before you feel better! Accept that. The critical thing, the most important action, is participating in the quest.

Start participating by giving up the fantasy that on day one, everything changes.

The Dreaded Side Effects

Once you're on medication, you are subjecting your body to chemical stuff it's not accustomed to. Your body says, Hey, I don't like this! Your body has, maybe, various unpleasant reactions. Some are a whole lot less fun—or more dangerous—than others. If you're getting drowsy all the time and your job is driving a truck, that's not so good. If you're feeling a little jittery and jumpy, maybe that's something you can live with.

So I urge you to take a clear reading of your side effects, maybe rate them on a scale of one to ten in terms of how seriously they affect how you go about your day. Are they so bad that they outweigh the good the pills are doing? If so, talk it over with your doctor and see what else is available for you or if the dosages can be adjusted. Are the side effects annoying, but basically you can kind of ignore them if you put your mind to it? Maybe you should. Nobody said this was going to be a walk in the park.

Here's what you may be up against:

dizziness	headaches
skin eruptions	blurred vision
fatigue, sleepiness, lethargy	sexual dysfunction
jumpy, jerky feelings	excessive thirst
weight gain	shaky hands
diarrhea	slowed-down thoughts
water retention	a lot of peeing
upset stomach	dry mouth
sweating	fluttery eyes
constipation	

Sounds terrible, right? Obviously, not all of these reactions are going to land on you at once and some of them you'll never experience at all.

Smart Medication Management

Okay, you've got your meds, and you and your doctor are fairly pleased with how things are going. But if, like many of us, you're required to swallow five, ten, fifteen pills a day, this calls for some management skills. Here are some suggestions that will be useful.

Read the inserts that come with the pills.

These are the instructions that tell you about this substance you're ingesting.

Now, reading through that teeny, tiny print and absorbing the message may give you a heart attack to go along with your bipolar disorder. They've got to tell you the "contraindications," and what just possibly might go wrong. Here's a sample of the kind of news you might hear: the drug you're about to take may cause blood in your urine and difficulty urinating, cause your bones to hurt and press on your spinal cord, contribute to paralysis (with or without fatal complications!), make you tired or dizzy, give you hot flashes, and lead to a reduction in testicle size. This last one is okay, because who wants to walk around with huge testicles? But paralysis with possibly fatal complications? Do you love it?

They have to tell you this stuff. Calm down, take a deep breath, and read through that teeny, tiny print again. You should find information you do need about how the drug may interact with other prescription medications you're taking, with certain foods, with common over-the-counter pills, or with herbal supplements and vitamins, and similar advice. You need to know these things. Ideally, your doctor will have gone over it all with you already, but inform yourself. I would even suggest keeping the little instruction pieces of paper with the tiny print in a special envelope or a folder, for access at some future point when you have questions about your meds or you're thinking you could use some more vitamin B or E in your life, and you want to know if that's okay. Besides, that effort contributes to your feeling of being responsible, participating in getting better, which is what you should feel.

Be watchful during any change of medication or dosages.

Pay attention to how you're feeling when you're introducing a new chemical mix. Listen to what your body is telling you. Write it down to discuss at your next doctor's visit. This might seem obvious, but a lot of people think, "Well, this is the same stuff I've been taking, just adding some more milligrams, no problem." There might be a problem.

Fit medication times into the routine of your days.

Did I take that damn pill already or not? A lot of people have a hard time remembering. Making it less complicated isn't all that hard. Buy one of those little containers that neatly sort out different pills according to day and time. Make it part of your ritual to fill up the boxes with a week's meds on Sunday night, or whatever your schedule is. Invest in an alarm watch you can program to send you a "ding" when it's time for your medicine.

But I also like the notion of making medicating yourself part of the warp and woof of your daily rounds, so to speak: In the morning, you start the coffeemaker, brush your teeth, feed the cat, pop your pills. In the evening, you load the dishwasher, put out the trash, wash off your makeup, pop your pills. Again, I think this serves the purpose of promoting acceptance and responsibility; bipolar disorder is part of your life, like it or not, and needs your attention, just like the cat and your teeth.

One woman found it helpful to put her medications out in little decorative containers. "When I was a kid," she recalled, "I went to live with my aunt and uncle for two weeks while my mom was in the hospital having an operation. This aunt and uncle were kind of health fanatics who took a huge handful of vitamins or dietary supplements every morning. Each night, my aunt would arrange the next day's pills in little cups next to their places at the kitchen table where we ate breakfast.

"For some reason, I just loved this routine. When I started my medication regimen, I bought a set of small, beautiful Japanese bowls, and I set out my pills in them. It looks less medicinal. It's like I'm taking vitamins or something to make my body more healthy, which of course I am."

Whatever works for smart medication management, and sticking with the program.

Which brings us to what I call the $10,000 question.

Should You Ever Quit Your Medications?

The short answer is: no, absolutely not. Don't even think about taking such a step before thoroughly discussing it with your doctor.

But why is quitting such a temptation?

The reasons are many: Maybe the pills are expensive. Or you have insurance nightmares, with a lot of required faxing back and forth of forms, and infuriating delays and confusion. Moving to a new city or state and having to connect with a new doctor can mean a medication regimen gets delayed, or the whole thing slips through the cracks for too long. Regular blood tests, if needed, are a pain. And, of course, the feeling-sorry-for-yourself stuff. One woman said: "When I find myself thinking this is so unfair, why do I have to live with this, I know I'm in danger of quitting my meds. Or conveniently 'forgetting' to take them."

> A bipolar friend of mine told me she stopped taking her medication because it made her fat. Then she said she was off to McDonald's for lunch. I said, "Is that where you left the pills that made you fat?" I haven't spoken to her in a while now.

Some people, like Matt, who's been in treatment for three years, suspect there's something unmacho about needing medication. "My whole family was like that," said Matt, "you don't even take an aspirin for a headache. You buck up, pull yourself together, grit your way through whatever's bothering you. Like if you took a Tylenol, you were a wuss." He reminds himself every day that he'd better overcome any lingering problem about popping pills.

There are a couple of legitimate reasons to get off the meds, in consultation with your doctor. If you're a woman wanting to get pregnant, you are advised to stop. If you develop a medical condition that isn't going to coexist with what you're taking, you might have to discontinue your regimen. If you had just one doozy of a manic episode in your life, you've had a year on the pills and all went well, and you have no family history of this illness, your doctor may agree to reduce the medication with the possibility that you won't need it indefinitely.

But those situations apply to just a small percentage of bipolars. And the rest of us come up with all kinds of justifications for why it really is okay, even desirable, to get those pesky little pills out of our lives. In the box on pages 102–104, I've listed some of the explanations/excuses we give ourselves. Most often, however, I hear versions of two arguments.

One: "The pills have made me feel bad because of the side effects, so maybe I should go off them."

Two: "The pills have made me feel great, so maybe I don't need them anymore."

Because I place staying on your medicine right at the forefront of getting better—because nobody's going to do it for you, nobody's going to put the stuff down your throat or drag you by the collar to check in with your doctor—I want to explore those arguments a bit.

The Side Effect Factor

You've read the teeny, tiny print—"important information you should know"—describing all the possible difficulties of the wonder drug you're taking. You've conducted your online research. And maybe, if you're lucky, you have a doctor who took the time to spell out some of the problems. So you have, supposedly, been informed and warned.

Nevertheless, those side effects can be traumatic if you experience them and they can start you thinking you'd really like to stop with the pills. The common ones are listed in the box on page 89. Nothing to look forward to, obviously.

With men, the number one traumatic side effect usually has to do with sexual functioning—specifically, the *inability* to function. When a guy wants to talk to me after one of my seminars, probably 75 percent of the time he tells me he went off his medication because of sexual side effects. I've always been able to relate to that, because it's one of the biggest issues I faced. And I was pretty floored. There I was taking antidepressants, and suddenly I was unable to perform with my wife. The equipment didn't work! I called my doctor and said, "Uh, I'm having a little sex issue here, and it's getting me kind of depressed."

The irony is, back in the bad old days, the main activity that once in a while kind of brought me out of a black funk was sex, or at least I was *less* depressed for fifteen minutes or so. Now, all nicely drugged up with antidepressants, I couldn't even get my fifteen minutes of fame. And that was depressing. Talk about your vicious circle.

Women have unwelcome sexual side effects as well. For many, however, weight gain seems to cause the most unhappiness, and there's another vicious circle for you. A woman with whom I swap bipolar stories regularly said to me once, "I used to be depressed and skinny. Then I went on medication, I got undepressed, and then I got fat. Being fat makes me depressed. So, don't you think depressed and skinny is better than depressed and fat?" She could laugh at herself a little. More important, she eventually focused on bringing her weight down through the usual methods, diet and exercise.

Doctors really could be a little more helpful, a little more informative about the dreaded side effects. Instead of remarking blandly, "You may experience some weight gain," maybe that doctor should spend some time saying, "Since you're going to be taking this and you may gain weight, here's some information on adjusting your diet, and here's the phone number of a gym in your area you might want to check out—people in our practice get a discount," and so on. Instead of, "This medication may have a sexual side effect," the good doc might want to go a little deeper on that whole thing. Because if you tell me that my manhood, bruised and battered though it may be (but still operational, thank goodness), might stop working, well, that's an important aspect of life. That ranks right up there with, do I have gas in my car?

Too many doctors don't take enough time going over these matters with their patients. Gird yourself for the possibilities, and take action.

Side effects may be alleviated or ended by changing to another medication. Some side effects can fade away once your body has adjusted to the meds, so time may be all you need. Talk to your doctor. And if he or she doesn't have the patience or inclination to talk, I say again: search out one who will. Don't assume you must suffer in silence. A good doctor will describe to you other meds that may work differently with your brain chemistry and get rid of the nasty symptoms you've experienced. The more you understand about side effects, the less blindsided you are and the less likely you are to go off your regimen. If you're expecting a sucker punch, you can prepare for it.

Figure out other ways to help yourself. I've had people tell me they read racy books with their spouse or watch romantic movies together and start cuddling. If that's what it takes to make sex work and stay compliant on your medication, that's what you have to do. Join a gym. Pay more attention to your diet.

Don't allow yourself to get thrown off the basically good track you're on because the pills have had some bad side effects.

The Feeling Great Factor

Perhaps the most common temptation for all of us who have turned the corner comes when the mood swings have diminished and life is sweet again. Things are going well, and that's when you decide, Maybe I don't need all this stuff anymore. After I've shared my stories of being in hell and then emerging from hell, someone almost always raises a hand and says, "Paul, it seems like you're doing so great, don't you feel as though you can get off the medications now? Or cut down on them?" That's something I hear repeatedly.

I try to answer that question with another one: if I'm diabetic, and I'm controlling my illness with insulin, and I'm not getting woozy and sweaty and feeling lousy anymore, do I stop taking the insulin? Well, no. Obviously, the reason I'm doing better is because of the medication, and I must constantly remind myself of that fact. The medication did not cure me of diabetes; it is going about the job of stabilizing me, providing a substance that my body needs in order to process sugar and other carbohydrates and that my body isn't providing for itself.

It's the same with bipolar disorder. We are not cured, but we are fortunate in being able to take a substance that will provide our bodies with something they need to stabilize our moods and allow us to function in the world.

When life is going well, that's also when you can start getting a little nostalgic about the old highs. In retrospect, those manic periods can seem pretty neat. Exciting. Going at life at full tilt. A bipolar friend said to me recently, "Man, I used to have so much energy, I was so jazzed. Some of the good things got blunted after starting with the meds." He's a musician, like me, and values his creative spirit and drive. I could relate to that, too. Yeah, those old highs were awesome. I made a lot of money. But I have to remember that I made a lot of my most massive mistakes then as well, a lot of really bad judgment calls. And in the long run, when I was manic was when, in turn, I *lost* most of my money. The awesome highs ultimately plunked me into a deeper depression than I had experienced prior to that.

Entertaining seven thousand thoughts at a time when I was

manic helped me write music. Staying up three days in a row is not an issue, and once your brain starts to be deprived of sleep, that's when a lot of the most creative ideas start flowing. And I was lucky, because very often I was surrounded by the right people, professional people who tolerated my craziness and who picked up the pieces as I was flinging them all over the place. People who could say, "Neat idea, hey, good song, nice line," and who would do the real nuts-and-bolts work of putting the ideas to use, which I couldn't do because I'd already forgotten them before I left the room.

But then: along with some good ideas, there was a lot of plain dreck that I turned out. Not that I realized it at the time. I remember once driving from my home in Cincinnati to Nashville and back three times in a twenty-four-hour period—heading there high as a kite with a new song in my pocket. Or actually, on a CD that I popped in the car player. I cranked the sound up, singing along to what was going to be my big hit, spending the money I was going to make on this one, credit cards about to be paid off, new Vette about to be bought, and on and on, my mind on fire and my soul flying high. That song lasted around four minutes; it took four hours to get to my manager's office in Nashville; so I probably sang that little tune, top of my lungs, about sixty times. Except for the minutes I was on the phone, calling everybody I knew, telling them my new hit record would be coming out soon, and oh, by the way, I'd love it if you quit your job to go out on the road touring with me, because I got to have my pals around. Phone call after phone call, all the way down.

Well, I left my CD for my manager to listen to, jumped back in my car, filled up the tank at the BP gas station down the road, and headed home. My cell phone rang. *Yes, my manager is calling and he needs me to come right back and sign a contract for that song.* "*Yel*-lo," I answered, because I was a supercool songwriter guy. No, it was my wife, Lisa, not having a clue where I was, because I'd neglected to tell her I was leaving town again, asking me to stay put and get some sleep. *No, no, this is our ticket to the big time,* I told her, *I'll be home in a few hours,* and I still remember clicking off the phone and in that *instant,* my mood and my life changed. From up to down in a flash. Not answering my phone. Hoping my car got hit by a truck.

That's how fast it can happen.

My brilliant hit song was the hit that wasn't. My manager hated it. Or, the way he put it was, "You brought me a coaster, man." A coaster is a CD that you might as well use to set your drink on, because the contents aren't good for anything else. As I recall, that little jaunt was also one of the many times that a stop was put on my gas credit card. They look at you funny when you're filling up two, three, and (once) four times a day at two stations in two cities a few hundred miles apart.

Do I miss the old highs? No, not at all.

Think it through. Talk it through with yourself or your doctor or your supportive friend or relative. I guarantee you, the bad stuff that happened during those periods outweighs the good stuff. I guarantee that you won't miss your highs enough to risk going back there. The trade-off isn't worth it.

The Medication Break: Good Idea or Bad Idea?

There's a part two to the temptation to quit your meds: should you quit for a while, now that you're better, just to see how you feel?

I have myself been without medication in the period since being diagnosed. The first cocktail assortment we found that actually worked for me did the job for about a year and a half and then it didn't. We were back to square one. At that time, I told my doctor, Steve, that I wanted to step down off the meds and be medication-free for thirty days, flush out my system with lots of water, eat salads and other good stuff. Be kind of a focused health nut for a month. But the clear understanding was that I was not quitting, we'd be initiating a different regimen, and I intentionally wanted to take that brief time to do what I thought of as cleaning out my body. Steve was willing to allow me to do that. He believed the risks were minimal. At the end of that month, I started on the new program, which worked like a charm.

Again, these issues are to be decided individually, between patient and doctor. Explore the possibilities.

A good doctor will want to discuss with you the risks if you start to relapse. He or she will review previous episodes when for one reason or another your regimen was interrupted, and how long it took for you to stabilize again. He or she might want you to check in on a more regular basis, to monitor what's going on.

So I am basically very boring on this $10,000 question: should you—could you—quit your medications? The answer is no. I'm not willing to do that, and you should not be, either. From all the information I have gathered and from the empirical evidence of my life, I know that if I stopped my medication, I would in essence be giving myself a death sentence.

What about down the road? Will I, will you, ever be drug-free, or are we on this plan for the rest of our born days? I don't know the answer to that. There's always hope. I like to think that somehow, someday my body chemistry may change and my brain will take care of itself. But it's the better part of wisdom for us all to assume that, well, yeah, this is for life.

A Few Other Reasons You Might Think You Have for Quitting Your Meds . . . and Why You Should Stop Yourself from Doing That

The arguments can be on the tip of your tongue or in the back of your mind, always tempting. Here are some of them:

"I've been taking the pills, but they're not working. What's the point?"

Have you allowed enough time for the benefits to kick in? It doesn't happen overnight. Remember, there's no "on day one, everything changes." Pills have a cumulative effect, especially if you've started off on a low dosage that will gradually be increased.

"A little touch of hypomania now and then makes me feel good, makes me work better, so maybe I'll go off the pills for a while."

Everyone likes feeling good and working better, but when you are bipolar, that little touch of unmedicated hypomania can easily and quickly jump to a full-blown manic episode or serious depression.

"I can't stand my doctor, so I figure what does he know?"

Find another one, definitely. You have to have a decent level of trust in and rapport with this individual. Or if you basically can't stand *all* doctors, put more effort into boning up on everything you can learn about this illness, so you can ask the right questions and, ideally, satisfy yourself that the M.D. you're seeing probably does know what she's talking about. Ask her if you can get a second opinion, and see how she reacts to that. She should say, "By all means."

I talked about this in the last chapter, and it's a big, big issue. According to those who research bipolar disorder, not liking the doctor is way up there on the list of reasons people ignore or forget about prescribed medications.

"Pills are dangerous, unnatural things. Who knows what the long-term effects will be?"

Letting your aversion to pills stop you from sticking with them is a huge mistake. Remind yourself that, sad to say, you *do* need them. Life without them is going to be worse, as surely you've learned the hard way. A good support group can be a good place to air these thoughts.

"I can't drink and take the meds, they tell me, so I'll just go off the pills while I'm on my two-week vacation in Aruba, because a guy's gotta have a little fun."

Here's the bottom line: stopping medication almost always results in a relapse, and that can happen within a very short

continues on next page . . .

continued from previous page . . .

amount of time, like less than two weeks. How much fun is that going to be?

> *"My husband pesters me about whether I took my pills today. My kids pester me. It's my life and I'll do what I want."*

Pestering relatives can be a pain in the neck, and in chapter 7 we look at some ways to encourage them, politely but firmly, to back off. But if you're careless about taking your medicine, or sometimes you just don't, in order to show them you're in charge, it's a little like cutting off your nose to spite your face.

> *"I don't believe in all this brain chemistry stuff. I can think of five other reasons why my life got screwed up."*

Sorry. The brain chemistry stuff is real. Stick with the pills to get the brain chemistry under control. Then, if you want, hash out the other reasons for your screwed-up life with a psychotherapist, a priest or rabbi, or a very wise, patient friend.

You Are Not a Doctor

This obvious statement deserves to be said out loud, even hammered home. Do not tinker with your dosages on your own. Do not prescribe yourself.

Suppose you're on the right mix, maybe after a lengthy process of trial and error. Then the right mix turns into the wrong mix. Or you're feeling more lousy than usual. Adjustments are called for. And suppose that several factors somewhat out of your control—you can't get a doctor's appointment, you have to go out of town—are interfering with getting that adjustment. By this time, you're thinking you know enough about which pills are doing what that you can switch things around yourself. This is almost surely courting disaster.

One woman was having unpleasant side effects, called her doctor, and, at his suggestion over the phone, upped one medication she was taking by 100 mg a day. This didn't improve things a whole lot, so over a long, restless weekend, she decided to add another 100 mg, while simultaneously cutting back the dosage on yet another pill she had been taking regularly. "I went from feeling jumpy, not able to sit still, not able to lie down," she said, "to crawling out of my skin. I was having visual distortions. I couldn't walk through a doorway without crashing into the sides. It was terrifying." She got herself to an emergency room.

Don't fool around.

SIX

"Nobody but You Can Keep You Well"

Staying Motivated, and Taking Your Bipolar Pulse

You're at that blessed place now where you know, at last, what's wrong with you. It has a name. You found a doctor who confirmed that you are not crazy, you have an illness and it can be treated. You have settled into the right medication regimen, maybe after some of that miserable trial and error I talked about earlier.

So this is it. You're on the right path, and you know what you need in order to keep in control. Just take your medicine, and you'll get rid of the mood swings and life will be good again.

Not so fast.

First, you may talk yourself into going off your medications, even if right now you'd say that'll never happen. The temptation can arise all too easily. We looked at some of the reasons many of us toy with the idea, or act on the idea, of stopping with the pills. They are powerful reasons. They get to us. In fact, *half of bipolar people on a lithium regimen do quit their meds*, some sooner, some later.

Second, there is always a possibility that your symptoms will recur, even when you're complying. The symptoms may be tamer, no spiraling wildly as in the past, but some of the familiar thoughts or feelings or behaviors start creeping in. Remember, we're not cured. We still have an illness.

Third, some of the same triggers that probably played a part in a manic or depressive phase in the bad old days may still pop up in your life. The same old people are there. The same old habits are lurking.

Frank, thirty-nine, says about his experience living with bipolar disorder, "It can be so fantastically all-consuming in a subtle kind of way that it can trip you at every turn, almost without your awareness."

He adds, "You have to get a handle on the whole picture, what you should have, what you should steer clear of. What you need more of, what you need less of. That's what keeps you in control and means you don't feel like a victim or that the meds are the only thing between you and going off the deep end again. You learn that there's a lot you can do for yourself." Frank is successfully managing his condition in various ways.

Yes, there is a lot you can do for yourself. Not only *can* you do it, you *must* do it if you want to stay healthy. But though we all have the same illness, self-regulation is an individual business. Personality has something to do with it. The job you have, the schedules you keep are factors. One shoe does not fit all. Finding your fit is a vital key.

Of course, if you're cycling into a serious depression or into an extreme manic phase, strong protective measures are called for, and I talk about developing a "what if?" plan on page 165. Some involve the active support or intervention of family members or close friends. The advice in this chapter will help you, I hope, during what I would call the normal blips or ups and downs of a mostly stabilized bipolar life. I want to share here a number of tools that many people, including me, have found useful.

Confession of a Bipolar Boy

Now, I have to fess up. It's damn easy for me to tell others what they need to do in order to stay focused and keep the course. It's no problem for me to get on a stage and talk to two hundred people about why they need to be on top of their illness. And yet sometimes it is very hard for me, myself, to live the way I am preaching, for lack of a better word. Sometimes even Bipolar Boy forgets and has to be reminded.

One of my fondest smacks upside the head came from my wife, Lisa.

It was a beautiful spring afternoon and I had just come home from the studio, feeling pretty crappy mentally. Depressed and filled with a lot of poor, poor Paul. We do that, you know, we feel very sorry for ourselves. At that point, I was getting pretty fed up with the whole search for the right medication mix. Now, most of the times when I decided to leave the studio early, I really believed I'd go home and do something with the kids, putter around the house. In fact, I usually made a beeline for my bed. Bed is home base for me, as I've said before. I'd pull into the driveway, and it was like my body was saying, "Hey, this is where that bed is. Let's jump right in it, you have nothing better to do with your life."

So on this afternoon, I walked in the door and Lisa was there, of course, with a smile and a kiss and "How was your day?" And true to form, I kept on walking straight to the bedroom, yelling out, "If anyone calls, I'm not home. I don't care who the hell it is, I am not home," and then I shut the door. This was my way of telling my wife and children, "Stay away from Dad, he's on the nut train right now and needs to be left alone." I got into bed and pulled the covers over my head and shut my eyes real hard. Talk about loony. I really thought that if I just shut my eyes hard, I'd go right to sleep. Never worked out that way.

I'm not sure how much time passed, but Lisa came in and out of the room every now and then, and each time she'd say or do some small thing. Though it was anything but small, as you'll see by the end of this story. Lisa has a way of getting me to stop and think, always has for some reason, without ever telling me what I'm doing wrong or giving advice. On one trip this afternoon, she touched my foot and walked out. I don't know why I remember that, but I do. Just a touch on my foot, as if to say, "I am not leaving you alone and I am here." The next time, she brought in a soda and put it on the table next to the bed, and left again. About an hour into my little sleepless nap, there was Lisa coming in and opening the window wide.

I love a cool breeze hitting me while I'm lying in bed, and I think she knew that. Maybe it's because I remember lying next to my father in bed, talking and the wind coming in. He liked it, too; he'd say, "I could stay here all day." Dad worked nights, so in the afternoon when I was coming home from school, he would often just be waking up, and I'd climb in there with him and we'd talk.

When Lisa threw the window open, I could hear the outside world. Me lying there with the covers over my head and not being able to see, all I had were the sounds. Cars in the street, birds, the blinds now hitting the window casing as the breeze blew them in and out. One sound I did not hear was happiness. I never heard any happiness when I was like that.

Then, just before she left the room, Lisa's hand came to rest on my leg and she said in a soft, warm voice, "You know, I could listen to her laugh all day." At that moment I heard our little Olivia on the swing set outside the window, laughing and laughing. Olivia is an incredible girl, sent by God without a doubt. Her laugh will get you every single time. There's something connected to her vocal cords that, when she laughs, makes you feel as though you're a thousand feet in the air.

As I lay in bed feeling sorry for myself, suddenly with Lisa's one comment now all I could hear was that laugh. It became louder and louder, and I found myself laughing, too. Olivia would giggle and I would chuckle. Soon, I threw the covers off, and I remember saying to myself, "What the hell are you doing, Paul?" I changed my clothes and walked outside and watched my laughing daughter.

I learned a lot that day.

As you're handling your battles, the normal ups and downs of a mostly stabilized bipolar life, every so often you, too, probably should ask yourself, "What the hell am I doing?" You have to pay attention to the direction you're going, and to not feeling sorry for yourself. Pay attention to the people in your world, the ones who help you see the good in things, and the ones who don't. Get your head around something constructive, actions you can take right there and then. Remind yourself that in order to get better, you have to actually participate—in your life, in your treatment, in regulating your illness.

What should you be doing to aid and abet the pills in the challenge of keeping stable and staying motivated?

Generally speaking, I think of this aspect of self-regulation as paying attention to the body and to the head, to what's below the neck and what's above the neck. Of course, especially for us bipolars, there's no such real separation, but it's a useful way, as my friend Frank said, of getting a handle on the whole picture.

First, what's good for your body? What do you need to know about healthful eating and drinking, and what are you going to do about that?

Second, what are you doing to keep track of the stuff going on in your head? Or, as I call it, are you taking your bipolar pulse, tuning in to the up-and-down blips that are still part of living with this disorder?

Paying attention, making adjustments and changes in the direction of better physical and mental health, helps keep your moods stabilized. Don't pay attention, and you're taking unwise chances with your life.

Self-Regulation and Your Body

There's a lot of information out there in our health-focused, even health-obsessed, culture about what makes for healthful living. It's no great mystery. Unless you've been living under a rock for the last couple of decades, you couldn't have missed it. Here's a rundown.

Eating, Drinking, and Moving Around

The National Institute of Mental Health, the Depression and Bipolar Support Alliance, the American Psychological Association, and other sources of advice and information have something to say about smart eating habits. In brief:

- Pick foods that are low in saturated fats.

- Whole grains, fresh fruits, fresh vegetables—they're all good for you.

- Fish is good for you.

- Binge eating is not good for you.

- Keep your intake of sweets in moderation.

- Avoid fried stuff.

It sounds familiar, doesn't it?
Sick or not, bipolar or not, common sense and countless

magazine articles and news bulletins tell us we all should be managing our diets and eating along these lines. But I do think that diet—exercise, too—in a perfect bipolar world must be a top priority, and we who have this illness should strive to understand the effects of certain foods.

I've learned by paying attention to how I feel that it's a good idea for me to stay away from too much coffee and caffeine, too much chocolate, too much sugar. My medication works best when I refrain from consuming a lot of those admittedly enjoyable things, because they tend to hype me up. And of course if weight gain is one of the side effects you're battling, maintaining a careful diet is doubly important.

Smoking is not good for anybody, as we all know. However, if you have a brain illness and you're smoking, unquestionably you are making things way worse. If you're puffing away all the time, you're causing that sick little three-pound glob of Jell-O in your skull to get even less oxygen—and function less well than it already does.

It's a goal of mine—and I am far from perfect in terms of reaching it—to stick with good foods and regular exercise and no cigarettes, not only because of my illness but because my body is deteriorating from one year to the next. It's the natural order of things! I try to keep active. I'll go ice skating. I'll ride the stationary bike I've set up in my bedroom. And then sometimes I won't.

I wish that I could say that exercise is something you should seriously consider adding to your lifestyle, but I cannot. Instead, I must say that diet and exercise are probably the single most important changes you *must* make in order to get a better handle on your life and your illness.

In November 2006, I was getting out of the shower right before going to speak. I realized that there was this huge, fat man in my room with me. Upon watching the steam evaporate from the mirror, I saw that this fat man was me. Little old Bipolar Boy had become big fat slobby boy.

I came home from that road trip with one goal in mind. I was going to be in size 32 pants and be back down to 180 pounds by the end of May 2007. That's right, I decided that I could no longer allow myself to look like the fat ass I had become. I haven't had a McCrapo burger since December 1. No fast food other than Subway has entered my body. I go to the gym at least six days a week, get plenty of water, and average five miles of cardio per workout day. I feel better today than I have ever felt in my life. I feel great.

If you are bipolar and you smoke, eat crap, and sit on your rear end, I have some very bad news for you: you are never going to get 100 percent better. Sorry to break it to you this way, but it is the only way I know how. Smoking kills your brain, crap food makes you fat and messes with your brain functions, and sitting around doing nothing makes all of the above way worse.

Now I know you are saying, *That's easy for you to say, Paul, you are doing better now.* You are right, it is easy for me to say; however, it was hard as hell for me to get to the point of being able to say it. I am only trying to help you here. I am simply trying to tell you the truth and the truth is, you have got to be better than you've ever been at taking care of yourself. Yes, it is hard to stop smoking, I know—it took me three real tries to actually do it. Keep trying, don't just stop because you fail or slip up. I also know how hard it is to get to the gym every day, but I have managed to only miss about nine days total during the past nine months, and I am on the road most of my life. Find a gym at the hotel; go to a gym in the town you're staying in. Most of them are willing to sell you a day pass, and you may even find, as I have, that a lot of them will say, Come on in and work out for free.

Bottom line: get to a gym, stop smoking, eat right, and for God's sake slow down, if not cut out, the booze.

Physical Exercise: Why and How

Here's what moving around does for you, according to research studies:

- Both nonaerobic (strengthening) and aerobic (heart and lung) exercises tend to reduce anxiety.
- Exercise cheers you up and lifts your mood. It is called "an effective but underused treatment for mild to moderate depression."
- Exercise boosts self-esteem and confidence.

Just the very things bipolar people need.

I call it "moving around" to emphasize the notion that you don't have to have fancy equipment or a gym membership or a swimming pool in your backyard. It doesn't have to cost anything at all. Doctors and therapists say a thirty-minute walk or light jog three times a week is excellent. If thirty minutes sounds like a lot, start with an even easier jaunt of fifteen minutes, suggests a smart physician: With your watch on, walk out your front door, he says, and walk for seven and a half minutes away from your house. Turn around and walk back. There you go. Exercise.

Can Bipolars Be Social Drinkers?

Obviously, if you have an alcohol or drug problem *and* a mental illness, there's a good likelihood that immediately stopping drinking or drugging should be an important and immediate lifestyle change. You will not be healthy as long as you are drinking to excess. Or smoking pot or doing other recreational or illegal drugs. Besides, using illegal drugs is, as the name says, against the law. It's a bad idea. Stop. Period, no matter what.

Often, someone comes over to me after one of my talks and tells me his treatments aren't working, he's not getting any better, his life is pathetic, and on and on. My first question to that individual is, Are you sticking with your medication? If he says no, I try to engage him in a little talk about why it's so critical to take his meds the way they were prescribed. If he tells me yes, he's complying with the regimen he and his doctor worked out, then my second question is, Do you drink a lot of alcohol or are you taking drugs? Because if that's happening, it totally messes up the ability of the medications to work as intended.

Alcohol and drugs affect the brain. That's how you get drunk, that's how you get high. Remember that you already have a broken brain, your brain already doesn't work. And by drinking or drugging, you're giving it another reason not to work *and* at the same time, trying to get it to work. That is a no-win deal.

Can a bipolar person be a social drinker?

Now, this might sound contradictory to what I just said. But I hope to God the answer can be, for some, yes, because I myself am a social drinker, with some precautions (which I'll get into in a minute). Certainly, I downed an incredible amount of alcohol during my battle in coming to terms with my illness. Today, I will go out and have a couple of beers with a friend from time to time, or a glass of wine with a restaurant meal. But I will be sure to pay careful attention to what I'm doing. An occasional beer doesn't seem to be a problem for me; more than that *is* a problem. I learned a practical lesson on that score.

When my wife and I moved into a new house a while back, everyone was in a celebratory mood over that weekend and margaritas were the drink of choice. I drank a lot of them in those two days, and I woke up on Monday not feeling good at all. I was depressed, and I just wasn't right for a five-day period after that. Lisa called me at work later that first day and asked if there was anything she could do to help me. Obviously, she saw that I was in trouble. I said, You know what? There's nothing for you to do, I did this to myself.

By that, I meant I knew—I had learned over the years—that I can't drink in such a manner, because my brain isn't like other people's. It can't take all that alcohol. Nowadays, especially since the weekend with the margaritas, I am way more conscientious about what I'm doing, because I realize that I am gambling with my treatment and my life. I have to understand that if I do go out and party with friends and have more than a beer or a glass of wine, I will pay a price. And a price higher than just a hangover. I am taking the chance of throwing my medicated brain into a place I don't want it to go.

Now, obviously if you're an alcoholic or a recovering alcoholic, the answer to the question, Can bipolars be social drinkers?

is going to be no. You're dealing with two different diseases: alcoholism and bipolar disorder. If you're not an alcoholic but enjoy an occasional social drink, you must be incredibly watchful and responsible. You must discuss this issue with your doctor, because some medications have zero tolerance for alcohol. And know that if you slip into excess mode, you are gambling with your treatment and in turn with your life. And if that's a gamble you're willing to take, then you've got a big problem.

Sleeping

Sleep is a biggie for bipolars. For one thing, it seems that, because of our broken brains, we may be more likely than other folks to have unstable internal clocks. The day and night rhythms are out of whack, which means that going to bed, falling asleep, and waking up the next morning don't come easily and naturally. So sleep problems are a symptom of our illness. On top of that, however, sleep problems—too much sleep, too little sleep—can also *cause* mood shifts and fluctuations. A vicious circle, symptom and cause.

For another thing, we can get kind of obsessed about the whole business. Maybe there are unpleasant associations from the past, a time when you were so depressed all you could do or wanted to do was sleep, and you're afraid of landing back in that place again. Or, the opposite: "I went through a period of a few months, when I was out of a job because of downsizing," said one woman. "I was getting depressed, and the funny thing is, you think when somebody's depressed, they just sleep all the time.

The problem was I couldn't sleep, and in my mind I just kept going around and around the same worries, which was making me feel more hopeless." For me, as I've said, bed was my home base for so many years, where I'd escape and pull the covers over my head and squeeze my eyes shut—and not sleep. In the grip of a manic phase, on the other hand, you can feel you simply don't need any. The thoughts are coming a mile a minute, the world is beckoning. I used to stay up hours upon hours during those times.

Thinking about sleeping makes us anxious about sleeping. We don't have a very good handle on what place this natural function occupies in our lives.

Some researchers did a study of bipolar people and their sleeping habits, and they looked at three things: how long it took the person to get to sleep, how often or if the person woke up at night, and how many hours of sleep he or she got altogether. Here's what they found: The bipolars greatly *overestimated* how long it actually took them to fall asleep. And they *underestimated* how much sleep they did get. Things weren't as bad as they thought!

So maybe we need to do a little less thinking and obsessing, while at the same time acknowledging that proper sleep is a critical aspect to staying healthy. Doctors tell us that too little sleep is a major trigger for manic episodes and too much sleep is a trigger for depression. This is important stuff. It's still my inclination to be a little manic, to stay up for those hours on end. Now, in a sense, I force myself to get the right amount of sleep—to make going to bed at roughly the same time every night, getting up at roughly the same time every morning, part of my routine.

Falling Asleep: A Few Tips

Keeping to a regular routine—this is when I'll get to bed at night, this is when I'll get up in the morning—is just part one. Actually falling asleep is the harder part for many people. If that's your problem, maybe one or more of the following ideas will help:

- Avoid caffeine, sugar, and tobacco for at least a couple of hours before bedtime.
- Get plenty of exercise, but avoid exercising for at least a couple of hours before bedtime.
- Don't eat in bed, or make phone calls or send emails from bed.
- Don't watch the late news on TV.
- To quiet your overly active mind, try meditation techniques, like focusing on deep breathing.
- Also for your overly active mind: Practice positive self-talk. Very intentionally, replace a negative thought that's creeping in with an optimistic, pleasant one.
- Get a "white noise" gadget that blocks outside sounds.
- Invest in some really fantastic bed stuff, like sheets and quilts.
- Pray.
- Check with your doctor about whether a sleeping medication is a good idea.

Self-Regulation and Your Head

By "your head," I mean what's going on mentally and emotionally. Paying attention to those realities helps you stay in control. Most important, get good at recognizing mood changes and the signs that you might be heading into an up cycle or a down cycle. Each of us has our own idiosyncratic way of keeping track. Here are some ideas about what works, for me and for others, in monitoring ourselves and our emotional environment.

The Company You Keep

Who are you hanging around with? Who do you allow yourself to be with? And are these people good for you as you're learning more about self-regulating, staying motivated, and keeping the course?

The not-so-good people may not always be the obvious candidates, pro or con. For some of us, they may be close to home.

Family, friends, and enemies

Family members can and should and sometimes *must* be knowledgeable and sensitive allies in your efforts to manage a life with bipolar disorder. Sometimes they can perceive a whole lot more accurately than you do what's going on with your behaviors, especially if you may be cycling into a manic phase—when you're feeling that's the normal you. In the following chapter, I want to share some smart ways these good folks can learn to be on the same page, to be empathetic supporters and maybe occasional loving watchdogs over your moods and treatment. For example, you may want to prearrange with them a plan of action, such as when it's okay for them to contact your doctor.

However, we're not all so lucky to have good people in our corner, or people who are able to understand and accept our illness. If you're not getting the support you need, then I think you would be wise to consider separating yourself, at least until you settle into a treatment regimen. Here's one woman's story.

For Vida, the teenage years and early twenties were the worst of times.

"High school was when I really started going up and down. I think the signs of bipolar were there even earlier, but once I was hit with all the normal adolescent stuff plus was a little bit more on my own in terms of coming and going, that's when I started losing control in a serious way. I spent time running around with wild kids in school, and my parents were freaking out, trying to ground me, all that.

"After high school, I enrolled in a community college. I lived at home and took the bus to the campus. Midway through my first year, I fell into a horrible depression. I missed most of my classes. Sometimes I would not change my clothes for several days, and I'd just sleep on the living room couch. One afternoon my mother came home and found me there, and she started pounding on my back, screaming at me to get up. If I had a child in that state, I think I'd immediately get her to a shrink, but that was not something my parents could do, not something in their experience or culture."

When she was twenty, Vida moved out of her family home, rented a room in a nearby town, and got a job as a cashier in a home appliances store. Life did not go well. She did a lot of bar-hopping, she befriended people unwisely, and, one terrible evening, she was raped in the car of a man who'd given her a ride back to her apartment. A coworker got her to a hospital emergency room, "and though I didn't realize it at the time," Vida says, "that was the beginning of getting out of my nightmare."

Vida was considered a suicide risk and was hospitalized for two weeks. She had the good fortune to talk to a smart doctor, then another smart doctor when she left the hospital. She's now twenty-four and has been on a medication regimen for two years that's allowing her to live a more stable life. She works, she maintains a small apartment, and she has plans to enter nursing school. What she can't do very comfortably yet is spend much time with her parents.

"They came to see me in the hospital, and I remember my father saying little and just glaring at me, with a look that said he thought I'd brought all this trouble on myself. Of course, that's sort of true, but I know now that my illness had something to do with it, too. They don't want to hear anything about bipolar disorder. And it's not even that I want to talk about it all that much. It's that I know they think everything I went through—and the sorrow I gave them—is because of some weakness on my part, some failing of character or willpower."

She limits her time with her parents for now to "meeting my mother somewhere for lunch every now and then, maybe stopping by the house on a weekend afternoon when I'm feeling strong and in control. I have to be careful not to let them rattle my cage."

That may be a smart decision on her part. We have to do what we have to do. We have to think about who is likely to rattle the cage, upset our stability, and whether or not doing the best for ourselves should include limited contact.

In my own case, I will no longer allow myself to be around

individuals who annoy me. Once I was a guy who hid in a closet and wouldn't come out because of my illness. Now I just don't go near certain people—I'll leave the room, I'll arrange my work schedule so our paths do not cross—because they make me sick, in a way. Not sick in a stomach-turning sense, but they're not good for me. They agitate me and anger me. As much as possible, I make sure I'm in the right places, the places I need to be in.

Give this some thought.

Who is maybe not so good for you right now?

A "friend" who always tries to cajole you into having a drink or staying out late to party when you're serious about sticking to a sleep routine?

A relative who thinks it's funny, or maybe helpful, to remind you—repeatedly—of exactly when, where, and how you screwed up in the past?

Someone who's a gloomy Gus, has nothing pleasant or hopeful to say about anything?

Someone who makes a point of stating that he doesn't believe there is such a thing as mental illness?

Be with the people and in the places you need.

Support groups

Many have found information and community in attending support groups, and I think those are wonderful for people who need them. I always say, hear as many bipolar stories as you can, because first, you feel less alone, and second, you begin to realize that you do not have a monopoly on any one way of living with our sickness. Hear other peoples' stories, and you might get some good ideas on what to do when you're in a rough period.

But I would issue a warning, and if you have stuck with me thus far, it will probably not surprise you: Certainly, bipolar disorder is a difficult illness to live with. But you can live with it. You *can't* live with it, not well, if you gripe and blame it for every problem in your life. Sometimes what's going wrong is bipolar disorder. Sometimes it's not. So beware of groups that indulge griping and blaming.

I'm not much of a support group person myself. That's partly my personality. I'm kind of mean. I'm pretty sarcastic and I'm pretty callous. I also have the great blessing and benefit of speaking about bipolar in my seminars, which are essentially my support groups. But I don't have room for lazy people and for those who aren't willing to help themselves. And from my own experience and what I've heard from others, a lot of times support groups are filled with characters who'd rather blame their illness for why they fail instead of doing something about failing.

I went to a group one time. People went around the circle and told their tales: "Hi, I'm Billy, I'm bipolar." Everybody said, "Hi, Billy." That kind of thing. I was brand new, so I just sat there and listened, and we came to one guy, and he said, "Hi, I'm John, I'm bipolar." The circle: "Hi, John, how are you?" John replied, "I had a rotten day. My company sent me home and I'm getting my pay docked, because I'm bipolar." The circle: "Wow, what happened?" John: "Well, my boss really pissed me off and I told him I was going to kill him. This guy knows I'm bipolar. So they sent me home." The circle: "That's so rotten, that's so unfair."

I raised my hand. I said, "I know I'm new here. But I just gotta clarify something. John, if I was your boss, number one, I would have had you arrested. And then I would have fired you. So my thinking is, they didn't send you home because you're bipolar, they sent you home because you told your boss you were going to kill him. You can't do that. That's just not it."

The circle looked at me with stony eyes.

I went home that night and my wife asked, "How did it go?" And I said, "Those people are crazy. All eighteen people in that room blamed their problems on the fact that they're bipolar."

It's hard for me to sit in a circle and deal with that scene. I don't buy it, I don't swallow that attitude very well. Maybe one reason is because my mother wouldn't allow us to blame our problems on other people or things. It is what it is because we allow it to be that way.

Support groups do work for many. I know there are excellent ones out there, and I've talked to a lot of men and women who've found great help, great benefit in a group. But I would advise you to pick and choose with care. Locate a likely-sounding group in your area, attend a couple of meetings, get a sense of the individuals—who they are, what they do, how they feel, what they have to say for themselves. Join a chapter of the Depression and Bipolar Support Alliance (DBSA) or of the National Alliance for the Mentally Ill (NAMI). There are a lot of them. If you get on mailing lists or email lists, you will learn about current developments concerning this illness and can tune in to all kinds of other useful information and sources of help.

You have to surround yourself with people who function well

in the world, people who are actually getting better and living with their illness. If you surround yourself with a bunch of individuals who aren't—if you're in a room with twenty people who don't have jobs, don't have insurance, don't have hope—you will not help yourself.

I will go a little further out on a limb here, and add this thought, which may not be a popular one: Do not hang out in bipolar chat rooms or read message boards online all the time. I have yet to find a chat room or message board that is filled with truly hopeful, encouraging stories. Most of what I've come across are a lot of people telling each other how miserable their lives are. Yes, we need to share our experiences, share what's worked and what hasn't in dealing with this illness successfully, spread helpful ideas. But what you don't need is to listen to a lot of bitching and moaning. It's not good for you.

How Am I Doing? Keeping Tabs

A friend who is in treatment called me and said, "I've turned down three invitations in the last couple of weeks. Nice events with some nice people, just casual get-togethers. But I haven't felt like going out. I want to stay home and hang out by myself and watch old movies. So I'm wondering about it, Paul. What do you think? I'm wondering if I'm starting to cycle."

I would name this another $10,000 question: am I doing what I'm doing because I have a mental illness? Surely, many people who are not ill might also turn down three invitations in two weeks, because they're pooped or they're not feeling particularly social and they prefer to spend relaxed time on their own. And they will not wonder and worry about it. But I understood where my friend was coming from.

We bipolars are always questioning whether we're having a rotten day because we're having a rotten day, or we're having a rotten day because we're sick. And in a way, that's kind of a bad thing; it has a downside. Once you start believing that everything you do is related to your illness or could be, once you start over-analyzing, that in itself will drive you crazy. Or work against you in a lot of ways, including using bipolar as an excuse: "I'm ill, so that's why I'm being mean to my wife or that's why I don't want to get up and go to work." The old blame game is very easy to fall into. Like John in the circle, who was convinced his pay was docked because he was bipolar, not because he said out loud that he wanted to kill somebody.

Still, self-questioning, self-evaluating is necessary.

There are various ways to go about it, starting from the kind of casual and informal, which is what I'll talk about here, and moving into the more structured, which we'll look at after.

For me, it's a natural and a good fit just to ask myself, How am I doing? Look at the whole picture, as Frank said earlier, and do it regularly. It's the practice of stepping out of your body, in a sense, and reviewing what's going on from an outsider's point of view. What have you been up to lately, pal? Are you eating the right foods, most of the time? Getting a little exercise? Getting enough sleep? Staying away from people you should stay away from?

I've always been blessed with that ability, of being able to step out and look at my life with a dispassionate eye. I do it in my car all the time—go over a matter in my mind (what's left of it) and talk out loud. Certainly it does get some looks when I'm driving along and talking to myself, but hashing it out that way in private has helped me sort out my reasons and the pros and cons.

I ask myself, If I make this decision here, if I take that particular action there, how is it going to play out? If I buy this piece of equipment I have my eye on, am I doing it for my business benefit or for the kick of spending? Why is this money going to be leaving my hands? One of the biggest problems for many people with this illness, and certainly it was for me, is spending money they don't have. Of course, most individuals in this country are doing the same thing, and they're not all bipolar. But we're different. So for me, when I mull over putting down a chunk of cash to improve my business capabilities, I've got to think it over: am I doing it because it really is the right move in a business sense or because I'm sick and I'm just spending money to try to make myself feel better? Usually, I can come up with an accurate answer.

Another thing: I know when I'm starting to feel as if I'm slipping into a funk, into a depression. If the feeling lasts a week or so, then it's time to check in with my doctor. But I do allow myself periods of being a little lethargic, maybe, without hitting the panic button. Because I realize that sometimes it's just life. For one thing, I'm in a line of work—the entertainment business—that leaves a lot of room for disappointment and rejection. So I'm obviously going to have days when it's just a bad, crummy, depressing day.

Keeping tabs is probably one of the most important parts of my treatment and how I self-regulate. I don't go to therapists; I'm not a big fan of individual psychotherapy with a professional, though I know it can be immensely helpful for many. That's just me. My speaking engagements are my therapy. I have my writing. And then there are those mornings in my car talking to myself.

Triggers and Warning Signs

In chapter 4, on getting a diagnosis, we had a rundown of the feelings and behaviors that help a medical professional decide that he or she is looking at bipolar disorder. Here is a brief recap, some signs that you may be starting to cycle into a manic or a depressive stage. Again, it's when you experience any of this in what constitutes for you an abnormal swerve from your controlled state—or when you know from the past that a particular feeling is a big red flag for you—that you may be heading for trouble. If you have become pretty good at taking your bipolar mood temperature, you'll figure out if the fatigue, impulsiveness, or whatever is a sign of cycling into an episode or just a natural and unsurprising response to something going on in your life at the time.

feeling unusually fatigued
   and lacking energy
bouts of insomnia,
   or other changes in
   sleep patterns
social withdrawal
feelings of grandiosity
loss of interest in formerly
   pleasant activities
feelings of sadness, crying
thoughts of death

feelings of guilt and
   self-criticism
endless worrying
impulsiveness
hostility
restlessness
risk taking
loss of interest in sex
inability to concentrate
changes in dress or
   grooming habits
overeating

Mood Mapping and Red Flags

Many advice books and treatment specialists recommend self-monitoring through careful, detailed, written-out lists or charts. And many people find those charts a good fit with their lifestyle and their personalities.

Tom, thirty-eight, describes himself like this: "I'm an obsessive, neatnik, bipolar certified public accountant." Tom likes to see things in black and white, right there in writing. He makes a connection between his bipolar disorder and his choice of occupation. "I always was good at math and I loved it. It made sense. I remember this back in school, that math was there, unchanging, sensible, I got it, and that was true when everything else in my life didn't make any sense to me. I like to look at a page of lines and columns and things going at right angles to each other. Thus . . . accounting!"

Tom has been on a medication regimen for five years, ever since he was diagnosed, and also puts great stock in keeping precise personal track of his moods. On his specially designed graph paper, marked off by hours, he notes at the end of each day exactly how he felt, what he was doing at the time he felt that way, who he was with, and other details. He's particularly concerned about indications that he may be slipping into a more manic phase, and he's "been around the block often enough," he says, to spot some of those signs. "One thing is, I will start talking to people too much, or maybe too loudly or inappropriately. I hear myself, and I can see that what I'm doing isn't going over very well with the person I'm with, but it's hard to get myself to stop."

It doesn't happen often, because his medications are working well and also because, he feels, his daily self-monitoring gives him a better grip on any fluctuations. "For me, when I'm starting to see I might be heading into a high, swimming is what helps. I get to my health club and do leisurely laps for an hour, and my mind settles down."

Many people find mood charts similar to the one Tom has worked out for himself to be great aids in self-regulation, a useful way to piece together patterns of behavior. In the box below, I've outlined some ways to set up one for yourself.

Mapping Moods: Charting Your Ups and Downs on a Daily Basis

Do a little checking around online or in medical guidebooks, and you're going to find a slew of suggested mood chart forms. Many of them look so dense and complicated that you can feel you're back in school, facing some unpleasant homework you have to get done. A chart is going to work—that is, it's going to convey useful information you can plug into your life—only if you keep it regularly and don't stress out over the whole effort. Locate a form that makes sense for you. Or design one that suits your needs and your style. Get out a sheet of paper (one paper for one month), a ruler, a pen, and start making some lines and boxes. These are the elements that typically comprise a mood chart:

- *Days of the month*, numbered from 1 to 31 along the left-hand side of the page, top to bottom
- *Your mood on each day*, entered in a second column beside the first

continues on next page . . .

---

continued from previous page . . .

You can name this second column your "Mental Health Meter" or "How I Felt" or just "Mood." Here you will note whether you felt normal or down (depressed) or up (manic). You may want to note if you were anxious, agitated, sad, angry, irritable, and so on. Many charts suggest rating the intensity of your other-than-normal mood on a scale of 1 to 3: 1 is *mild*, nothing too bad going on; 2 is *moderate*, fairly intense, but you were still able to work and go about your daily business; 3 is *severe*, you were seriously affected to the extent that you weren't able to work.

The remaining columns of your chart should shed light on why your mood was fluctuating up or down that day, and consequently, on adjustments you probably should be making or situations to try to avoid in the future. This will be revealed by:

- *Eating and drinking.* You may want to make columns on your chart that say "breakfast," "lunch," "dinner," and you will put a check mark indicating that you did in fact have those meals. If seeing no checks reminds you that you have skipped breakfast and lunch for three days in a row, that might be a factor in your mood fluctuations.
- *Exercise.* Have you been getting any? Yes or no.
- *Sleep.* Have you been getting too much or too little?
- *Medications.* Did you take your prescribed meds? Yes or no. Here you should also note any changes in your prescriptions. You might want to spell this out in further detail by making a column for each one of the medications you take on a daily basis.
- *Stressors.* This is basically "stuff going on this day." Note anything out of the ordinary: Your boss chewed you out. You went to a party and didn't get home until 2 a.m. You got a big raise. You had a fight with your sister. And so on.

All these elements can be refined, redesigned, reworked to fit your unique bipolar personality and life, and I have seen many one-of-a-kind versions of mood charts. One man had a special column for "cups of coffee consumed," because he knew too much caffeine was his temptation and his problem. One woman had a section for "weight," because she was aware that a gain of a couple of pounds set off her moods. Some people have devised weekly charts for themselves, finding that to be an easier way to understand their up-and-down patterns.

If you're not going to keep it going, a mood chart won't be much help. Find what will work for you.

The Life Story Diary

Mood mapping may not be your cup of tea.

Holly, a thirty-seven-year-old self-employed woman who runs a small mail-order business out of her home, said, "Maybe I should keep one of those charts; it might not be a bad idea. I know it does people good, and more power to them. But to me personally, it's like focusing on the negative. Myself, I'd rather not think about what's gone on in terms of me being in a bad mood or a low mood that day or that week. I try to stay with the positive. And I don't have the patience for a chart."

She did take one action that helped her identify her triggers. "I decided to sit down and write 'The Story of My Previous Life as a Madwoman.' I had been pretty stabilized for a while, but I thought, let me write about that woman, before I was on meds and got smarter about a lot of things. I always enjoyed writing. I always kept a diary as a kid."

She spent about a month writing her "life as a madwoman" story, and asked her mother and her sister for their input. They remembered episodes that Holly did not, or that she recalled only in a hazy way. "I wrote it out in the third person, just intentionally to give myself a little distance. When I finished, I put it away for a while, and then I took it out, read it over, and thought about what it was telling me. I made notes in the margin with a red pen. My red flag notes." Her red flags looked something like this:

Don't do well when I'm under a deadline.

Routine family arguments make me more agitated than anybody else in the family.

Big crowds are not good for me.

Very blue around the beginning of spring.

Evening phone calls are better than morning phone calls.

Watch out for sleeping too little for a few days and then sleeping a weekend away.

Gardening and baking are my best distractions when I'm feeling down.

There was more. None of it was a total surprise to Holly, but the review reminded her of vulnerabilities and triggers that were part of her makeup. It reminded her to be on the cautious or watchful side during certain interludes or in certain situations, and to make time for her pleasures, like working in the garden or baking a cake, when she felt a little down. She also gave a list of her red flags to her mother and her sister, her "personal support team."

All of this is good. Anything that helps people out is a good thing.

I encourage you to try various techniques or self-regulating treatments to take your bipolar pulse. Again, find your own fit and then give it time to work and to inform you. A lot of individuals, myself included, will try a plan for two days or five days, and then let it fall by the wayside. That's not enough. If you're going to keep a mood chart, for example, do it for at least a couple of months, and see if that helps you get a better handle on how you react to different situations. If it pays off, then it's for you. But the most important thing is, stick with any new way of tracking your moods. Commit to the time.

When a Little Therapy Can't Hurt

Many people with this illness have spent time on the therapist's couch over the years. Maybe not literally stretched out flat, staring up at the ceiling, describing dreams, while the good shrink sits behind jotting down notes and saying nothing—but showing up once a week for the fifty-minute hour and talking about problems. And after a lot of hours of having the psychiatrist or psychologist ask questions like "How did that make you feel?" many chalked up the whole business as a waste of time. They didn't get better.

But there are various and fresh approaches to the traditional "talking cure" (which, in my opinion, is usually paying someone to listen to you gripe and feel sorry for yourself). In the box on page 139, you'll find a shorthand description of some of these. It might be worth your while to check out therapy if you have family issues that need to be smoothed out, or for other reasons.

For example, maybe you think you could benefit from concrete suggestions on how to think and act more "normally." I am using that word "normal" because after living in bipolar hell for so long, you can forget what normal looks and sounds like. Or you have gotten yourself into some ruts that you'd like to get out of, but you're having trouble doing that on your own.

Here's one woman's experience. Delia is fifty-three and was diagnosed and medicated correctly about three years ago. She also made a couple of big adjustments, including cutting out the alcohol that she had been using to self-medicate. She said: "About a year ago, I started thinking, 'Now what?' For all those years I tried to live very quietly, very low-key. I avoided new things. It was fearfulness, fear of setting off a bad episode and landing back in the hospital. I didn't have much fun. It was really an emotionally constipated kind of life. And now I'm feeling pretty good, but it's like my social talents got retarded somewhere. I'm self-conscious around people. Still overly cautious. I go into situations anticipating the worst."

Delia decided to figure out how to join the normal world, and landed with a behavioral therapist who immediately started helping her turn around destructive thinking and develop better social skills. "She gives me assignments, such as calling a person I'd like to be in contact with again or volunteering somewhere once a week. These are small goals that don't overwhelm me. The next time I see her, we talk about how that went. We also work on changing a negative thought to a positive thought. So when I think, 'If I stay for coffee hour after the church service, no one will talk to me and I'll be standing there alone,' I try to turn that off right away and switch it around in my head, and I tell myself, 'I'll go to coffee hour and stay for a few minutes, see what's going on.' This actually works." She's now considering joining the therapist's skills group that meets once a week for a couple of hours at a time.

How Therapy Works with Bipolar Disorder

If you are comfortable with the idea of therapy and think it might contribute to your getting better control of your bipolar symptoms, consider adding to your recovery tools some appointments with a therapist. Professional folks say that psychotherapy is especially useful in treating a tendency toward recurring bouts of depression. It's less effective in reviewing and reversing manic experiences and behaviors. There are four types of recommended therapy, each of which tackles issues with slightly different desired results:

- *Behavioral therapy*, as the name suggests, aims at encouraging you to change certain behaviors in ways that decrease stress and increase more satisfying and enjoyable reactions, which ideally will help cheer you up.
- *Cognitive therapy* works at correcting pessimistic thinking, those negative thoughts that pop into your head (somebody says, "That's a great dress!" and instead of feeling pleased at this nice remark, you think, "Sure, great dress, but I'm so fat, I can't wear jeans anymore").
- *Interpersonal therapy* gets you talking about how living with this illness may be straining personal relationships, and what to do about that.
- *Social rhythms therapy* helps you get regular routines, especially sleep patterns, on a stable footing.

continues on next page . . .

continued from previous page . . .

The American Psychological Association is a place to get more information and recommendations.

Therapy might be a saving grace if you're not getting the support you need from family and you want some ideas on how to improve that picture. If you are a bipolar person married to or in partnership with a "sane" person, hope and pray that he or she is understanding, and willing and able to take the journey with you. I am a fool and have done many stupid things over the years, and my wife has stayed right there—no matter how hard I tried to push her away. Well, sometimes maybe not *right* there, but she never traveled in her mind and heart to a point where she could no longer see me. That made all the difference. So I'll go out on another one of my limbs and say, if you do not have an understanding relationship with your partner, either fix it or end it. Life is too damn short to fight all the time, and if you have bipolar disorder and your relationship is crap, you're only adding monumental pain on top of mental illness.

Stopping the Cycle

Suppose you recognize that you *are* cycling into a depressive or a manic episode—then what?

If you feel you're getting a little too depressed and for too long, remember what works for you to help get you out of that mood. Distract yourself with the enjoyable activities in your life, like Holly who went out to her garden to dig in the earth for an afternoon or into her kitchen to bake something. A friend of mine told me, "I spend a few hours watching old Marx Brothers movies.

They always crack me up, no matter how many times I've seen them. Hey, when you're laughing, things don't look so bad."

One woman said this: "I start having obsessive thoughts about dying, not that I'm going to kill myself, but that I will die, and that seems to translate into imagining things going wrong with my body. Actual pains. However, I am perfectly healthy physically. I know from my history that if I keep on that negative track, I get into a seriously depressed frame of mind. So when I find myself obsessing that way, I'll set up lunch or dinner dates for every day of the week, go out and spend time with some friends. The point is not to be on my own, in my own head for too long. When you are with other people, and you make the effort to fix yourself up and look good and get out and talk to people about restaurants or vacations or books they're reading, that cheers you up." A little more exercise, which gets those good endorphins going in your brain, works for a lot of folks.

Heading into a hypomanic or manic phase is trickier. That's because you may be the last to know what's going on with you, or to recognize the signs. Since you will greatly benefit from the support of others—in fact, maybe desperately need it—I'm going to discuss those actions in the context of "we're in this together," in the following chapter.

People ask me all the time why I'm doing well. I say, first, that "doing well" is a relative business, and I have struggles every day just like everyone on this planet. I mention some of the ideas I've touched on in this chapter. And then I add that to do well, we all have to come up with our own answers.

If there's one point I want to come back to it would be this: there *is* a lot you can do through self-regulation to help yourself, but what works for you won't necessarily work for me, and vice versa. Too often doctors lump us together, and prescribe and advise on the basis of one illness, one treatment. That may be possible with a class of cancer or a type of diabetes or high blood pressure. But with the mental illness of bipolar disorder, each of us is one of a kind.

SEVEN

"We're in This Together"

Living with Someone Who's Living with Bipolar Disorder

In the old days, people would often say to my wife, "It must be terrific to live with a comedian," and, "Paul is so much fun to be around." Little did they realize just what Lisa was around. She didn't know which Paul was in the house or on the phone from one day—one hour—to the next.

My wife, my kids, my mother have been affected by my illness way more than I have been, in reality. Those folks have gone to hell and back with me. They did not ask to be on the train, but I took them anyway. And today, they can do nothing to *make* me stay healthy. It's up to me to take the meds and, in those other ways we talked about in the last chapter, be active in maintaining my mental wellness. It is up to *you*, my bipolar friend. At the same time, family members or other close companions really must become informed allies, to the best of their capabilities. This is the journey of a lifetime. You're not out of the woods yet, and in fact, you never will be. Those family members and close companions are accompanying you on the journey through the woods. And at times, they may see more clearly than you are able to just what's going on, especially if you may be starting to cycle into a manic phase.

So I'm addressing this chapter to the support team, those wonderful people who care about you, a bipolar spouse or relative or friend, and want the best for you. These are some of the most amazing individuals on the planet, because if they are husbands or wives or parents, they have typically been keeping the home front together, all the while watching a terrible thing happen to a loved one. That cannot be easy, no way, no how. Even when the bipolar is into recovery, it's a tough job the support person has, because being appropriately supportive calls for maintaining a tricky combination of cool-headed objectivity and loving concern. Plus, this woman or man has a life of her or his own. She or he wants to live it and deserves to live it. She or he should not feel as if 96 percent of all the energy in the relationship is being sucked into the needs and problems of a mentally ill person. That kind of feeling is going to wear anyone to a frazzle or lead to resentment and bitterness.

The suggestions I offer are presented, very roughly, in three categories, or correspond to three stages of participation in the life of someone with bipolar disorder: first, the time before finding out what's wrong; second, the time after the sick one has been correctly diagnosed and is starting out on treatment; and third, the maintenance life, with the possibility—which always must be considered—that everyone is living in the calm before another storm when the bipolar person is mood cycling and maybe heading toward a relapse. Some bits of advice apply across the board. Others concern particular circumstances during the journey.

You, diagnosed bipolar person, are paying attention to triggers and warning signs, keeping your mood chart, and making all those other good efforts at self-regulation. You, support person, are adjusting to your role. From my own life, and from hearing the stories of hundreds of sickies and their supporters, there are a number of useful, in fact, critical, dos and don'ts. I name them here.

Before Diagnosis

Our candidate for bipolar disorder may not have seen a doctor or is insisting nothing is wrong, but those nearby know something is, in fact, very wrong.

Inform Yourself

In my experience, this is the toughest situation: the sick individual is not at the point yet of seeking out real help, and the relative or friend is at wit's end—maybe puzzled, uncertain, definitely worried. These are the people who come, in large numbers, to hear one of my talks, and they are probably one of the hardest groups for me to speak to, simply because I have never been on their side of the fence. My wife and my children are my support; I am the supported.

For them, I pull out the facts and figures about bipolar disorder, and I tell them my stories—because in so many cases, they really do not know what the illness is or what it looks like from the inside out or what it can lead to. When I start describing the nutty things I've done and the black holes I've been in, I watch their faces literally drop to the floor. I hear them saying to themselves, *Oh, my God, Bill did that or Jane did that or Joey is doing that same exact thing or acting like that right now as we speak.*

Then, and only then, I think, do they understand that this illness is very serious, and their loved one is not faking anything or just "going through a rough time" that will soon end; it is a common illness with real issues and problems; people can get better, but getting better takes a hell of a lot of work and time. Most important, they are able to see that I got through it and my family did.

If you are in that worried place right now, if you know something bad is happening but you are not sure just what it is, inform yourself. Reading this book is informing yourself. Go further. Hunt up a talk or a seminar if there's one being held in your neighborhood, listen to some stories, get a realistic sense of the journey you are on, whether you want to be there or not. The one you care for and worry about maybe doesn't want to hear any of that right now, but you can and you should.

Try to Get Your Loved One to a Doctor

Who wants to be mentally ill? Nobody. Who will do anything and everything to avoid hearing that sentence landing on him? Your average individual with bipolar disorder, that's who. It is one of the great tragedies of this sickness that people choose not to learn what's wrong with them, or they delay learning until, as I've said before, they end up in the hospital or get fired from the fifth job in a row or in some other way must finally acknowledge the wreckage of a life. Or until the pain and misery are just too overwhelming.

As a worried, caring relative or friend, there are limits to your influence here; you can't really drag him by the ear to the doc. In addition, the more emphatically you insist that your loved one needs mental help, in a hurry, the less likely in most cases you are to succeed in getting him to admit it. Maybe you can be a little sneaky about it.

Jess, the mother of seventeen-year-old Johnny, was increasingly concerned about her son, to the point, she said, "of getting really panicky. This kid was really hyped up, not sleeping for a couple of days at a time, running up to strange people on the street and talking to them, all kinds of weird stuff. My husband was saying it was just teenage exuberance, hormones, all that, until even he started to think something serious was going on. I think the turning point was when Johnny's friends stopped coming around, they kind of steered clear of him." She was desperate to get her son to a doctor. "I decided my best hope was to persuade Johnny to see his old pediatrician, a very gentle and wise man we all liked a lot. He'd kind of outgrown this doctor and hadn't seen anybody in a long time. I called this doctor, asked if he could see me privately, and I went in and told him what was happening. I gave him all the background, all the specifics that I wanted him to be aware of if I could get Johnny to his office. Back home, I said to my son, very casually, offhand, 'Honey, why don't you go see Dr. Reagan for a checkup? You haven't had one in years, and I think they require one before you get to college.' Whether that was true or not, I had no idea. But Johnny agreed."

The boy and the pediatrician talked for a long time. That office visit, set up through a bit of subterfuge, was the beginning of Johnny getting the help he needed.

Another woman watched her husband sinking into deep depression, seemingly losing the will or energy to take any action for himself. She remembered: "Finally, I said to him, 'Phil, you don't look so hot, you don't have your old pep, I bet you're anemic or something. I'm going to make an appointment with the doctor, there's probably something you can take. You know, maybe you need iron pills.' I guess this sounded nonthreatening to him, not like I was saying he was a head case. I said I'd go with him and he said okay. Thank God for that visit, because the doctor right away started Phil on medication and he began to come out of it."

This serious illness of bipolar disorder needs medical attention. Do what you can to get it for your loved one.

Starting Treatment

The big road bump here for a bipolar is adjusting to the medications that are prescribed. But there's also the matter of coming to terms, practically and emotionally, with the fact of being mentally ill. Which actually may be the bigger bump.

Be Sympathetic . . . Constructively

Or maybe we should call this section, "Offer tough love."

Many bipolars say that, especially during the early stage of beginning treatment, some people in their lives react in really, really annoying ways. Said Ruth, "My husband and kids have been pretty okay with the whole business, and it has been tough because the medications weren't working for a long time. And I've had to make some lifestyle changes that didn't thrill them, like I am not going to be on call at any hour of the day or night for a drive to the mall or whatever. On the other hand, my mother, who lives with us, believes I'm making the whole thing up. When I try to explain to her what's going on, she doesn't listen. In her generation, I guess, there was no such thing as manic depression."

At the other extreme, said a woman in her mid-twenties who shares an apartment with her father and sister, "everybody is walking on eggshells around me, like I'm going to jump out the window at any minute. If I am in my room with the door closed for longer than ten minutes, I hear my dad come and stand outside. Trying to hear if I'm still breathing, I guess. Then after lurking there for a while, he taps quietly on the door and he says, 'Everything all right in there, Sherry?' My sister is almost as bad. She wants to micromanage my life, when I'm going out, where I'm going, when I should be back. If I wasn't already nuts, those two would make me nuts."

The get-over-yourself attitude, the walking on eggshells, and the micromanaging of loved ones are not easy for a bipolar to live with. At the same time, Ruth is the first to say she's aware that *she* was not a hell of a lot of fun to live with for a long time, and she's grateful for the accommodation shown by her husband and children. Sherry knows her family "roommates" care about her and worry. Still, the adjustments on everyone's part take effort.

When wrestling with new medications, settling into acceptance of a serious illness, and generally trying to get healthier, the bipolar person can act very touchy about what others say, for one thing. For another, she may prefer to say nothing about what ails her or, on the other hand, be unable to stop going over and over her problems, out loud, like poking at a chipped tooth with your tongue.

These are sensitive times.

So, to you amazing, wonderful support people, I offer a few suggestions of "what to say" and "what not to say" to a bipolar person who perhaps is still in the early stage of treatment.

Do Say

- *"I love you, I'm here, you mean a lot to me, I may not understand everything you're going through, but I care enough to try."*

Those are words that can never hurt. Your loved one may not *hear* what you say, may not really take it in. Just keep on, and eventually maybe bits and pieces will get through. I am also a huge fan of the good, old-fashioned hug.

- *"Is there anything I can do to help you find a good doctor?"*

Or to learn more about the pills? Get a second opinion? Do some further research? Locate a support group in the area? People who are suffering like sympathy. Some like pouring out their sad tales to a willing ear, and some enjoy it a little too much and too long. These are the feeling-sorry-for-themselves folks. My advice is, lend the sympathy and the willing ear for a while, but don't allow yourself to get turned into the therapist or the everlasting shoulder to cry on. That way, nothing moves forward. You also don't want to come across as the fixer, the one who's going to make it all better, which you can't do in any case.

What you *can* do, after listening to the sob story for a while, is offer to be of aid in steering the individual toward a positive action. He may shrug off your helping hand, but it's constructive to bring the talk around to a mention of useful stuff he could be doing. Some bipolars have to be urged to knock off their endless litany of complaints.

Do Not Say

• *"I know just how you feel."*

Unless you have been to bipolar hell and back yourself, you *do not* know, and it's a little offensive to the sufferer to hear those words.

• *"Don't get so down on yourself. Just look at all the good things you've done."*

This is a well-meaning effort to jolly the bipolar person out of any explanation he's attempting, any unpleasantness he's conveying, about his illness. It's well-meaning, but usually misguided, because the sick guy may have to or want to acknowledge what is so bad and so wrong. He may be way far off from the clarity of mind and the ability to focus on what's good about himself, and he doesn't want to hear the bad stuff swept under the table, as if it never happened.

For me, the jollying-up effort, which I got from a lot of friends, drove me crazy. Maybe I had done a few worthwhile things during the miserable period of my life, written some decent music, made some people laugh, did some fund-raising. But what I saw—and *all* I saw for a long time—was the drinking, the affairs, the lost money, the depression, the mania, the dangerous stunts. Don't tell me how good and great I am.

- *"Listen, things could be a lot worse."*

In another attempt, probably, to make the bipolar individual feel better, this remark is often followed by references to two or three other people the speaker knows who are suffering from a terminal illness or died at a young age or in other ways have or had sad lives. Things certainly could be worse than having bipolar disorder. But comments like this tend only to stir up feelings of self-recrimination. A woman at one of my talks said, "It's like telling a child, Eat up all your dinner, think about all the starving kids in the world. It's a guilt trip laid on you."

- *"Modern medicine is so wonderful, with all these fabulous drugs, you'll be better in no time."*

The reality is: there is no cure; medications are great but not the be-all and end-all; and, truth be told, not all who suffer from bipolar disorder are going to get better.

"I get that it's hard for people to understand how difficult it is to adjust to a medication regimen or find the right one," said Amy, thirty-seven, who has been in treatment for about a year, "but I've heard this kind of remark from several relatives when I've told them I've been diagnosed with manic depression, and it's irritating. It's this quick-fix mentality. My immediate temptation is to launch into a whole explanation of the pills, the side effects, the tests, and nobody wants that whole story.

"People want to put this upbeat spin on what's wrong with you, but it's not always what you need. It's like telling a woman who's just had a miscarriage, 'You'll have another baby, don't worry, all will be well.' It trivializes the whole experience. How do they know anyway? Maybe all won't be well."

Hold On to the Long-Range Picture

The early stages of treatment are devilish. Chances are your loved one may feel even worse than he did before. Almost certainly, it will be weeks or months before the good effects are apparent. There may be a lot of jiggling around with dosages and combinations before the mix is found.

This is often the hardest time, when the initial optimism of knowing, okay, this is what's been wrong and now we know what to do about it, gives way to discouragement because nothing seems to be improving. Be patient. Urge patience.

Going Down the Maintenance Road

The maintenance road, as I'm calling it, is when the bipolar's moods have been stabilized, and life is looking a lot more normal than it has for a long while, if ever. This is time to discuss, calmly and rationally, the fact that everyone is on a bipolar journey of a lifetime, and it would be a good idea to do a little planning and anticipation about what comes next. It's a time to consider any lifestyle adjustments that might help the journey run smoothly. It is *not* a time to breath a sigh of relief: *Whew, that's over with, now we can all go back to what we were doing before.* It's not over with.

Express Your Concerns and Fears

This is maybe not the first thing you want to do when things are on an even keel. But I think it's absolutely right, natural, and even important to explain at some point to your loved one what's on your mind, or what emotions you are coping with. "Negative" emotions, like worry, anxiety, and anger, are as normal as the pleasant ones, and when you clamp down on them they fester and get really poisonous. You're human, *you're* not sick, you're on a train that you didn't choose and you wish hadn't come to pick you up, and you're not a saint.

I'm no big fan of psych-talk, but the familiar recommendation from therapists to use "I" language makes sense, like this:

"I have to admit, I get pretty scared when I think that maybe the medication is going to wear off after a while."

"I don't want to be nervous all the time, I don't want to over-react to little stuff, but I sort of can't help it right now."

"You know, I think I'd feel a little more relaxed and reassured if I could go with you once or twice when you check in with the doctor, just to see if I have any questions he might answer." You can express your feelings without being judgmental or accusatory.

A woman whose husband was diagnosed with manic depression during their engagement supported him in every way while he went into treatment, and the two got married at last. Emma, in her mid-thirties, said a rough time in their relationship came when he wanted them to have a child and she wasn't so sure she did. "We had always talked in the past about having a family," she said. "But after all we'd been through with his illness, I had a different feeling about that. My mind was in another place, where I saw us living a different kind of life, no kids. I love Peter. I'm committed to him, but I don't think I want to bring a child into this, for several reasons. I was adjusting to that, and he wasn't."

It was hard getting him to appreciate her worries. "He's highly intelligent, but on this issue, it was like I was attacking his manhood: of course he could have a child, of course there wouldn't be a problem, love would conquer all. I didn't agree. I stuck to my guns."

They took that issue into marital counseling with a therapist who knew a thing or two about bipolar disorder. At last report, it was still being hashed over. But I think this woman was right to stick to her guns and not ignore something important that was on her mind. I think it's right for a support person to air worries or anxieties concerning living with someone who's living with this illness. Of course, if you're constantly freaking out, wringing your hands, getting your stomach tied in knots, that's not great for you or your loved one, and maybe you should talk things over with a therapist. Or take up meditation. Buy one of those yoga mats and sign up for a course at the Y. But my point is, bipolar disorder in the relationship should not be the elephant in the house, where everybody knows it's there, but nobody says so.

And then there's anger. This is a tough one. Most of the support people I have talked to—almost all, really—are generous, loving folks who want nothing more than to move forward in health and stability. But the past is the past, history is history, the slate is not wiped clean just because this person in your life is taking some pills and feeling better. One woman, married for twenty years to a man finally diagnosed with bipolar disorder, said that the majority of those years were horrible: "My husband is doing okay now. But for all those years, I had so much to deal with. He was drinking heavily off and on. One morning I walked out toward the kitchen, and I saw his legs sticking out around the corner. He had passed out on the floor, broken his arm, and he couldn't get himself up. I didn't want our kids to see him lying there, and I dragged him out to the couch. Then to the hospital.

"I was the one who held on to a job. He was in and out of jobs. I paid the bills, I saw that the kids got to school and had their birthday parties. Now he's got steady work, thank God. Our two girls, they're teenagers now, love their daddy, and he's just eating up all this schmoozy feeling. Sometimes I think he doesn't deserve that. What do I want? I guess I want an apology. I want him to acknowledge all the stuff he put me through, even if he was sick and couldn't help it. I want him to say that he knows how hard it was for me. That I should have had a happier life, or I expected to anyway." Sometimes, she said, she feels a surge of such anger that she leaves the house to go and sit in the park for a while.

What do you do with all that rage and disappointment? I don't know. Get to a support group. Get to a therapist or a minister or a good friend who'll listen and let you vent. And maybe it's possible to ask for that acknowledgment, even thanks, from your bipolar loved one. Not by saying, "You sicko, look at this mess you've made of our lives, no wonder I'm a basket case," but in a planned, calm, nonconfrontational conversation: "I'm glad things are going well now, but I'm carrying around a lot of old anger, and it would help me if I knew that you realized and appreciated all the efforts I've made over the years to hold our family together."

That kind of calm, nonconfrontational talk isn't so easy to pull off, of course. For a lot of people, it's more possible with a third party in the room, a professional couples or family therapist who will steer the back-and-forth dialogue constructively and stop everybody from throwing punches. Maybe you need to find somebody like that. I said before, if your marriage or primary relationship is rotten, fix it or end it. If you don't know how to fix it and can't or don't want to end it, you must get counseling help.

Encourage Your Loved One to Continue Medication

Compliance is up to him or her. However, take a look again at chapter 5, on medications, and see the list of all the arguments why it's so tempting for a bipolar to be noncompliant. "The side effect factor" is always a pain, but maybe even more dangerous is "the feeling great factor," especially when it's combined with side effects. This one does typically hit when everybody's well along on the maintenance road, and the bipolar starts thinking, "I've been really okay, better than ever, for a year and a half now. Maybe I can quit or cut down on the meds, and maybe that will help me drop some of this damn weight I've gained."

Almost always, according to everything I've learned about this illness, medication is for life. It cannot be eliminated or reduced, at least not without careful monitoring by the doctor. If your loved one says out loud, "Maybe I can quit or cut down," reply, "No, dear, that's a bad idea. Let's make an appointment with your doctor before you take such drastic action." If your loved one hasn't said any such thing out loud, but you see he's not sticking to his regimen, say, with that cool-headed objectivity, "I have noticed, dear, that you're not sticking to your medication regimen. That's dangerous. Let's make an appointment with your doctor."

There's also just plain carelessness. Depending on the kind of character you're living with, you might have to be the pill police, making sure he remembers to pack up that little container every day.

However, there's a danger of crossing the line and nagging, pestering, and watchdogging, and someone who's responsibly paying attention to his meds will really hate that. I understand where you, support person, might be coming from: *He's going to forget to take his lithium this morning and then everything will come crashing down.* But nagging and pestering can have a rebound effect: *She treats me like a child, I'll show her, to hell with my morning pills.* I hear this one often from bipolars, the complaint that a support person is always looking over his shoulder, on his case. If that's a problem where you live, try to work out some arrangement that will both relieve your anxiety and let your loved one be in charge. Maybe he can agree to tell you, "Pills, check, done!" in the morning so you don't have to ask, and everybody is happier.

Maintain Household Routines

If you've never been one to stick to a lot of rigid plans about daily stuff, like when dinner gets on the table and when the TV gets turned off because it's time for bed, it might be extremely supportive now to try to get everyone on relatively set routines in these boring little ways. Bipolars have a lot of trouble with normal body cycles, like going to sleep, waking up, and eating. We're just not good at naturally regulating ourselves, we have to work at it, and when sleeping, waking, and eating are occurring randomly and all over the map, we tend to get a little jittery and irritable, overstimulated by our surroundings.

Keep to a schedule as much as possible. This is a lifestyle decision on which I think kids can be brought in very effectively: "Kids, you know that it's important for Dad to get to sleep on time, so from now on we're going to want you to do quiet things in your rooms after nine thirty. You can read, listen to your music, play a computer game, but keep the noise down and don't come running out to ask for something unless it's an emergency." If they've been living in the corners of bipolar hell for a few years, those children are probably relieved that life is ticking along smoothly and are happy to help keep it that way by making their own small contributions.

Plus, if drinking is a bad idea for your partner, and it almost surely is, maybe it's time to have no alcohol on the premises for anybody. Just a thought.

Beware of Lifestyle Stressors

Studies have demonstrated that individuals with bipolar disorder take longer than most people to snap back or regain equilibrium after a real-life stress.

There are the biggies: a relative dies, someone gets seriously sick, someone loses a job. They can't be avoided. But others, the smallies, probably can be, if you pay attention and know that certain situations, certain experiences, certain individuals tend to get your bipolar loved one in an agitated or gloomy state.

Holidays can be tough—for lots of people, and maybe doubly so for us bipolars. There are people in my life who make my blood pressure go up, who make my body chemistry change in bad ways. I still haven't figured out the reason, though it's probably some deep-rooted, selfish reality. What I have learned is that when my blood pressure goes up, my mouth starts moving and I say things that would be better left unsaid. So I've figured out that the best way to prevent damage is to stay out of those situations.

For example, on one recent Thanksgiving morning when we were invited to a family gathering, I said to my wife, "I need to stay here. You and the kids go and stay the whole day, come back about ten, and we'll all get along great." Because I knew that with other complications in my life over recent weeks, this was not a good year for me to be celebrating Thanksgiving around people. My typically short fuse was even shorter, and I did not want to take the chance of spoiling a holiday because someone said something that just ticked me off and started my mouth moving. My wife and kids went out to the planned dinner, I stayed home and watched *Apollo 13* a few times in my den, in the dark by myself with my dog, and I was happy. The family came home that night, we all stayed up talking for a while, and everybody was happy.

There's a lot of this kind of relatively simple accommodation you can make for your loved one. Don't push social get-togethers if she's clearly opposed to company at the moment. Be conscious of how seasonal changes affect her. We moody types tend to be overly sensitive to the times of the year, and many bipolar people are prone to an increase in depressed symptoms during the cold months with short daylight. Can you knock off for a few days in the winter, pop down to the Caribbean, and let everybody soak up some sun? There's a nice idea.

Stress can come in the wake of something good happening, not just bad stuff. One stressful time for a lot of bipolars is when starting a job or taking on suddenly greater job responsibilities. A woman who works in the magazine business jumped to a managerial position that placed lots of new demands on her, like going to regular meetings with the company brass and entertaining advertisers. "In the office," she said, "I was firing on all cylinders, mind going a mile a minute. Then I'd get home to my husband and my daughter, and feel leaden, mentally and physically. I just wanted to get in bed. I started rapid cycling pretty seriously over the course of twenty-four-hour periods." She needed to de-stress at work by keeping her eye on immediate goals and not trying to impress everyone as the second coming. At home, her husband/support person kept up a stable routine and schedule. For one thing, he saw to it that his wife didn't sleep for fifteen hours on a Saturday, which was what she wanted to do, but stuck to relatively regular sleep patterns.

You should be aware, too, that those *unavoidable* life stressors may send your loved one into a lengthy period of disequilibrium, or they might hit her harder than everyone else in the family—especially if they land in multiples. The pet cat died, part of the roof blew loose in the storm, and a grandfather fell and smashed his hip. Everybody feels upset and sad, but *she* keeps on heading down and down. These are the times it's vital to maintain routines and watch out for increased signs of agitation or depression, with possibly the need for checking in with the doctor.

Get a Little Support for Yourself

I'm talking not so much about groups that are out there, that you go to once a month and share stories. I'm talking about something closer to home. Is there a relative or relatives or a family friend who would be willing and able to share the great burden of being supportive to your loved one with bipolar disorder? And I will call this a great burden, because especially during active or unstabilized stages of the illness, responsibility weighs heavily on your shoulders. What I have noticed again and again as I talk to people is that typically there is one person in the bipolar's orbit— a spouse, a sibling, a parent—who takes on the major support role. Others in the orbit may be aware of the situation in general, but they're kind of on the B team, not called into active duty. Or maybe they're in the dark, they haven't been informed.

Not everyone is blessed to have a relative or family friend who can be counted on to understand what bipolar disorder is all about, to react in sensible ways, and to be genuinely helpful. Find out if you do. Share the news. Get support.

Here's one woman's story. Carrie, thirty-eight, has three brothers, Hank, Sam, and Neil. Hank is five years younger than Carrie; the other brothers are older. "When Hank was in his early and mid-twenties," Carrie said, "he was in terrible shape. For some reason, and I'm not sure how it all evolved, I became his caretaker. He had a job, he had his own place, but he went in and out of functioning normally. I brought him food, gave him money, and once got him to the psych ward in the hospital when he was so depressed he could hardly move. I was afraid he would kill himself. He stayed there for five days. My other brothers weren't in touch with him and didn't know anything about all this."

The hospitalization convinced Carrie that she needed to share the responsibility. "Hank was opposed to my saying anything, but I felt it could no longer be his decision. I called Sam and Neil, told them what was happening, and two days later they were both in my house, though they live pretty far away. We got Hank over here, and we had a four-way family meeting that lasted for several days. One brother went to Hank's apartment, cleaned it all up, and came back with piles of his unopened bills and other stuff. We opened it all, organized it, worked out a budget. We set up a new bank account for him and put a couple thousand dollars in it, to get him started. Neil called around to doctors and we found one who turned out to be great and, in fact, was the first person to say 'bipolar disorder.' In the beginning, Hank was, I think, pretty ashamed about this intervention, I guess you could call it. I think he was a little mad at me, but he got over it. Because by that point, he was scared about his life. At the end of those several days, we were all hugging and crying over a couple of pizzas."

Hank got better and is doing okay. The brothers remain on his support team.

My point is, if you are soldiering on alone in your support role, maybe that's not so healthy for you and maybe you don't have to. Many people with a bipolar loved one say nothing, don't reach out. If you don't reach out, you'll never know who the good guys are. When I shared the news of my illness, a couple of individuals I thought would get it in fact ran the other way. A couple of others, surprising me, stuck right by me, and they are here still.

Make a "What If?" Plan

This is kind of like a reverse living will—instructions not about "What to do to let me die" but "What to do to keep me alive and well." In a calm, quiet, mood-stabilized time and place, you and your bipolar relation should come to a mutually satisfactory agreement, maybe written down on paper, about when and under what circumstances you will man the bipolar front lines. You are saying, "If you, my loved one, begin acting in an ABC manner, we agree that I will take XYZ steps." These steps might include the ones listed below.

This is an emotional, thorny, just damn hard thing to accomplish for many bipolars and their support people. First, it's saying out loud that the bad times might return, and even if we are aware of that intellectually, it's upsetting to plan for it. Second, someone who's got his life back hates the idea of putting another person in charge of it. It's like, if I've been doing suicidal stuff in my car for years (behavior I personally know a lot about), and now I've got both hands firmly planted on the steering wheel at ten and two o'clock, I know where the brake is, I'm sailing along at a sane and legal fifty-five miles per hour, how is it going to feel to say that someone else, sooner or later, will be permitted to take my car keys away from me (which, in fact, might be part of your "what if" agreement)? It's going to feel lousy.

So the whole effort calls for tact, common sense, empathy, and cool-headed objectivity. However, if you and your loved one are well informed and have accepted the possibility of a relapse or cycling into episodes, this kind of agreement will be viewed as a smart cautionary move. It's like buying an insurance policy; you hope you'll never have to use it, but it's nice to have it there.

The first part of this "what if?" process should be knowing and naming what typically happens when the bipolar is in an unstabilized state, or what kinds of things tend to send him there. If he's been keeping a mood chart or a diary or being religious about following some of the self-regulation techniques we talked about earlier, he knows what to watch out for—the triggers and red flags—and you and he can review that information. But you and he both need to acknowledge that if he's cycling "up," you might see the signs and he won't.

Bipolars usually can spot when they're slipping into depressed states: they withdraw from people, feel fatigued, lose interest in things they've always liked, have crying jags, maybe brood about death, and they remember those behaviors and feelings. Usually, they know that is time to get to the doctor (to have a blood test, adjust dosages, add another med) or to do something pleasantly distracting and life-affirming, as we discussed in the last chapter. Manic phases, however, tend to elude self-recognition. There's actually a word for this—anosognosia, which is from Greek roots and means to not know a disease. Even with all your loved one has been through in the past, it is one of the sneaky, deadly aspects of bipolar disorder that he can lose perspective and objectivity. He's riding high, and he thinks everyone else is nuts.

In the box on page 171, I have quoted the words of a number of support people who recognized the early signs of a manic cycling episode. Maybe some will sound familiar to you. Maybe the picture is a little different with your loved one. All these red flags, however, involve changes in normal functioning, or in how the bipolar individual in his stabilized state usually talks, sleeps, thinks, and behaves. When any of this is going on, it's probably time to take some of those predetermined steps.

Here are a few suggestions for how your "what if?" agreement might sound. And again, every situation is unique, so the steps need to be tailored to fit your reality. There are two goals: one, to head off any crash-and-burn dangers, and two, to get your loved one some necessary help.

- *"We agree that I [support person] will call Marcia and Patsy, your best friends who know all about your bipolar disorder, if I think we're heading for trouble and we should get their opinion."*

The idea here is, you tell your loved one that she's getting a little too hyper; she says you don't know what you're talking about, you're just trying to control her life. This happens a lot. She should agree, in your "what if?" arrangement, that she will listen to the informed observations of some other people she trusts and doesn't have a big reason to be suspicious of.

- *"We agree that I [support person] will be the voice of reason regarding any money matters."*

Wild and crazy spending is a very common symptom of manic behavior, and a huge amount of damage can happen in a short time. You want to make sure your loved one doesn't announce he's just signed on to buy three motorcycles or a vacation house. People work out various arrangements to control the money thing: you will keep a separate checking account to which he doesn't have access and that will allow you to keep paying the monthly bills, you will be the cosigner of any investments he decides to make, he will turn over to you his credit cards when he's spiraling up, or other possibilities.

- *"We agree that I [support person] will decide what's best for the kids until I'm confident that things have gone back to normal."*

Maybe it's better for everyone if the children stay with the grandparents for a week or two. Or have sleepovers in the homes of good friends. Kids can get rattled and upset when one parent is starting to act a little peculiar.

- *"We agree that if you come up with a big, exciting idea of how we should change our lives, we will put that big, exciting idea on ice for at least two months."*

Here's another thing that happens a lot. Going into a manic mood, your bipolar loved one feels that anything and everything is possible, and he can make it happen, no question. This is when he suggests you should pull up stakes and move to the south of France, buy an IHOP franchise, or quit your lousy jobs. In this calm before a possible storm, you both agree that no immediate actions will be taken; two months down the road, when ideally he's on more stable ground, the hot idea probably won't sound so hot anymore.

- *"We agree that I [support person] can contact your doctor if you will not and if I'm feeling really concerned about you."*

It's a difficult agreement to reach: what is "feeling really concerned" going to be, what are the guidelines? It is also probably the most critical piece of the "what if?" agreement, because getting an adjustment in medications is the one thing that will stop the mood escalation, and that's likely the last thing the manic bipolar wants to happen. This has to be worked out in a three-way collaboration—bipolar individual, support person, doctor. For one thing, the bipolar patient may need to sign a form agreeing that his doctor may release or discuss information relating to his condition.

Depending on individual circumstances or past history, both parties—or all three parties, patient, support person, and doctor—might also need to agree on what constitutes an emergency, a dire situation in which the well-being and safety of the bipolar person calls for immediate hospitalization. A relapse can escalate very, very quickly.

I have heard sad, miserable stories from support people who watched loved ones cycle into dangerously manic behavior, with a feeling of helplessness as if watching a train wreck unfolding. Vickie, forty-three, said her husband, Bruce, had stopped taking his medications, "and things got very bad over the space of a week or ten days. He finally said he would go to our internist. I went with him. In the doctor's office, Bruce acted and talked in a bizarre, crude way. It terrified me. The doctor was sitting behind his desk, and Bruce put his feet up on the desk. Then he got up and walked around, picked up some framed photographs, and commented on the doctor's family, saying the wife was 'a real babe.'

"We took a cab home, and he ordered the cab to stop at one point. He went running into a store that was selling what looked like fake Oriental rugs and came out ten minutes later with this rug under his arm, which he said he had to give to his secretary because she didn't have a rug. That night, I did something out of panic. I gave Bruce a couple of Tylenols and a large glass of Scotch. I just wanted him to sleep, and I guess I had some absurd hope that when he woke up, it would be all right. Of course, it wasn't. I learned from someone in his office that he would show up for an hour and then leave. Bruce came home one afternoon with four new suits he had bought for himself.

"He had a membership to a club in Midtown. One evening I was home alone and I got a phone call from the manager. Bruce was there, and he was attempting to remove some plaque from the wall. According to the manager, Bruce was saying there were only two things in his life that he loved, his wife and this club, and he needed to take the plaque with him and somebody on the street had told him that was all right. I think at that point he was psychotic."

The next morning, Vickie called her husband's parents. After

A Little Manic Music: What Support People Report

Something you should know: these signs, signals, red flags may occur over a space of one week, two weeks, a month—or within a couple of days. Spotting them can be both scary and hurtful for you as support person, because your bipolar relative may seem to be rejecting all your good efforts, acting as if *you're* the problem in his life, pushing away loving overtures, telling you to butt out, or in other ways rejecting everything you do and stand for. Remember, he is not entirely in his "right mind," so to speak, and it's nothing personal against you.

Here are several ways that support people have recognized when a manic phase is coming on:

- "He gets incredibly snappish. He starts thinking everybody else is a complete dope, dumb, doesn't know anything. And he tells them as much."
- "She doesn't want anybody to talk to her. She's in a witchy mood."
- "He'll decide he's going to clean out the garage, paint the fence, rewire all the lamps. There's supplies all over the house, everything's in an uproar. He's running around trying to do it all at once."
- "Sex, all the time. That's what she wants. She kind of vamps me, comes on to me in these sort of embarrassing ways. And I'm supposed to be in the mood."
- "My wife starts planning elaborate parties. She starts calling up all kinds of people, even ones we don't know very well, and wants to invite them to dinner."
- "I know he's getting hyper when he comes out with insane ideas on how we're going to get rich beyond our wildest dreams."
- "He will get way less sleep than normal, but he says he's not tired."
- "He starts talking very loudly and very fast. People give him odd looks. He doesn't notice this."
- "She'll get suspicious, even a little paranoid. If we're in a group, she'll think a couple of people are talking about her."
- "Sort of saintlike. A little beatific smile on her face. Like she sees all, knows all, can solve all problems and save the world."

conferring with his psychiatrist by phone, the three of them took Bruce by private car service to a residential facility in a nearby suburb. He was treated there for two months.

That was five years ago. Bruce is being properly medicated and stabilized, and has had no further episodes. But Vickie says now, "I wish I had taken action sooner. It can happen very fast, the relapse. You have to act."

Know When to Cool It, Relax, Back Off

I wrote in the previous chapter about how it's important for us bipolar types to get a handle on "normal" mood fluctuations. That's a message for the support team, as well. I'll have a day or a week when I'm feeling down, pissed at the world, want everyone to keep out of my way. And maybe that's because the world just kind of sucks at the moment: it's been a tough couple of months, money is tight, things are lousy on the job, whatever—and any nonsick person would probably feel equally down or mad, having a lousy day or a lousy month. That's life. The corollary to this observation concerns feelings of having a *good* day or a good month. Maybe things are going great, and any nonsick person would feel happy, all's right with the world. That's life, too.

Taking one's own bipolar temperature in this way calls for practice, thoughtfulness, experience, and talking things out with yourself. It's tricky. What I hear a lot in my talks, however, is that often the sick person is doing fine differentiating "normal" mood changes from potentially dangerous ones, while her support person or people are hypervigilant, jumping on any behavior that hints at trouble.

As somebody once said, "Sometimes a cigar is just a cigar." Sometimes a blue mood, an angry flare-up or argument, is just that, and not a bipolar episode about to rear its ugly head. Sometimes you need to relax and back off.

Above All, Love

Mark and Mary, a Florida couple, run a wonderful, genuinely supportive support group for people with this illness. Mark is not bipolar; his wife is. Here are these two amazing people living in their own little bipolar hell, and yet they spend many hours helping out others. Knowing some of the details of what they've been through over the years, I was curious about what it took for this man to be accepting and selfless. What it took, frankly, for him to remain with his wife through all the difficulties of diagnosis, medicating, staying focused, and watching for mood swings. One day I asked Mark, "Why do you stay?" His answer: "I love her."

His simple words had the effect of helping me appreciate my wife, Lisa, more than ever. Or put it this way: I understand her better than ever. Over the years, I'd often asked Lisa why she stuck around, and her reply was always the same, and those same simple words: "I love you." I could never quite accept that. Not until that conversation with Mark could I actually see it.

My final thought and advice in this chapter is directed to my bipolar reader. When your loving support person is telling you

"I love you, I care, I'm here for you," open your ears a little more and let those kind words sink in. We who are sick with bipolar disorder have to listen a little harder than normal, I think. And the people in your life who are saying the words must indeed love you a lot, because I feel pretty safe in saying that if you are sick right now, chances are you're being a pain in the ass. As much of a pain as you are, these people need you, they want you to be healthy again. They do not want you to leave, move away, push them away, or die. They want you to get better. They're willing to help. Let them help. Say thanks once in a while.

EIGHT

"You Have to Educate"

What Family, Friends, Bosses, and Coworkers Need to Know (or Not)

To tell the world you have a mental illness or not to tell. That is the question. Obviously, it's a question with quite a few possible answers. "No one in my company knows I'm bipolar," said Jerry, a thirty-nine-year-old manager of a retail store, "and I've mentioned it to only two close friends, who had kind of figured it out anyway. It's a huge effort keeping up that front, staying under the radar. At the same time, and this sounds crazy, it's easier there. It feels safer."

For many with this illness, whether to tell or not to tell falls somewhere between buttonholing strangers on the street to share the news and staying totally under the radar. Me? My license plate reads BIPOLAR, so that shows where I come in on the spectrum from "tell all" to "don't mention it to a living soul." Telling others about my illness I consider a matter of educating them about bipolar disorder, and I see that as part of my mission. I educate through my talks, through conveying facts and statistics, and also by the way I handle my life and my actions.

This chapter will shed some light on just why so many bipolars feel it necessary or wise to maintain the front, to not tell. The simplest explanation is, who wants to be mentally ill? Nobody. Then, without hammering home my own opinions, I hope to persuade you that informing others—in a nonthreatening, unscary, neutral way—is valuable, for a few reasons. First, *you* need to accept your illness, even embrace it, if you are going to survive and get better. Keeping any reference to it hidden away, like a dark and disgraceful aspect of yourself, makes it so much harder to accept and embrace. Yes, nobody wants to be mentally ill, but there it is, and it's not a disgrace. It's part of who you are, and shouldn't be any more embarrassing than having a high cholesterol count or a broken hip. Besides, you have a lot of company, maybe most of it under the radar: According to the Centers for Disease Control and Prevention *one out of every two people in the United States will have a diagnosable mental illness this year*. Doesn't this tell us that mental illness is or should be the number one health issue we face?

And yet, we don't want to talk about it. So this is the second reason for telling: People—many of them, anyway—do look at you funny when they know you're mentally ill. They shouldn't. They need educating. They need to lose their fear and suspicion. On my website, I say that I am committed to fighting the stigma *one mind at a time*. And the stigma is still there, make no mistake about it. Supposedly everybody's enlightened now: we're not crazy, we're not lazy, we have an illness. But start listening, and you'll realize that words like "schizo" and "demented" are still tossed around, that comics still poke fun at "the nut jobs," that TV talk shows land on any negative news about the possible side effects of treatment while offering little in the way of positives. No lingering stigma? I don't think so.

The enormous taboo that still, in this twenty-first century, exists around mental illness is a terrible thing, and it prevents sick people from seeking help because they don't want to be labeled, they're afraid of losing a job, or they don't want others to look at them funny. The stigma should be eradicated, and if we all cannot change policy and funding and institutionalized prejudice, we can each, at least, influence one person here and one person there to lose fear and suspicion. One mind at a time.

Sometimes, something terrific happens. A friend explained it this way: "People start coming out of the woodwork. When I let it be known to some friends that I was in treatment for bipolar disorder, and it was obvious that I wasn't a weirdo and a danger to society but a man who was calmly taking better control of his life and wasn't afraid to talk about all this, I started hearing from people. Somebody I knew slightly would take me aside or call me and say, 'I think this might be what my wife has' or 'I've been really worried about my brother, but I'm afraid to tell him he should see a doctor,' some version of that. It made me realize how many people do live in the shadows of mental illness."

Finally, educate others because even with all the love and good intentions in the world, the people in your life may simply not know how to "deal" with you. They may be overprotective or overreacting or wary or in their own form of self-protection and denial. They need information, as well as reassurance at times, and that you can give them.

Deciding Who to Tell and What to Say

The first rule on this one is there is no rule. Each and every individual with bipolar disorder is a little different from the next guy, because each life is unique. What is said or not said therefore is going to be handled differently.

Here's a suggestion: Get a pad of paper and write on the top the name of the person you're wondering about—should I tell or not? Make two columns with the headings "reasons to tell" and "reasons not to tell." Write down all the ideas that come to mind for each category.

For example, I'll make up this little checklist for my mom. The reasons I should or want to tell her would sound like this:

She's my mother.
She's been worried about me, I know.
She's always been a good listener.
I owe her an explanation for why I've been so distant.
I think she can give me advice; she's a wise person.
I could use her help and support.
She dealt with Dad, and I'm pretty sure he was bipolar.

Under the "reasons not to tell," I'd probably come up with just one:

I don't want to worry her.

Now, under your two columns, make a space to write down the worst-case/best-case scenarios if you spill the beans.

What is the worst that can happen if I tell my mother?

She will call me on the phone a lot to make sure I'm okay, and that will bug me. (Actually, that's not so terrible, I can always ask her to please not call so often.)

What is the best thing that can happen if I tell my mother?

I may learn more about how she handled the situation living with my father. That will give me insights about my own experiences, and it'll provide ideas I can share with Lisa and my kids.

My conclusion: yes, I'll tell Mom what's been going on with me.

Do your own exercise and see where it leads you. Though I'm all in favor of educating people by speaking out, disclosing the fact of your illness may be inviting trouble or complications with some individuals in your life. If the worst-case scenario clearly outweighs the best-case scenario, that's one place to stay under the radar, at least for now.

When you do speak up, maybe there are a few general rules after all.

- *Whatever you do say, run it through your mind a couple of times to see how it sounds.*

This disclosure, since it may rattle the person you're telling, should not come as an impulsive, ill-considered outburst.

• *Choose an appropriate time.*

Most likely you won't want to drop your news in the middle of cheery dinner party conversation, but neither do you have to go into a major, "I have something huge I need to tell you" buildup. You're not announcing the end of the world.

• *Emphasize the positive.*

Lead off with it—you are receiving treatment and you're going to be getting better. The words "mental illness" are scary, but you don't have to use those words necessarily. For that matter, you don't have to say "bipolar disorder," if that sounds like too much, too fast. You can call it a condition that causes your moods to go up and down a lot.

• *Do not make a ha-ha, jokey reference to what's wrong with you.*

Something like, "Yeah, the verdict is in, I'm officially a mental case, surprise, surprise!" This effort to make light of the situation will make you sound bizarre and truly scary.

• *Be prepared for a variety of reactions.*

Everything from "Holy crap, that's terrible" to "Me, too!" to "Really? Tell me more about it" to the blank stare, no reaction at all. The blank stare is kind of the worst, but I figure that's that guy's problem, not mine.

- *Be prepared to allow some time for your news to sink in or be truly accepted.*

Bipolar disorder is a medical condition that needs to be treated, partly anyway, through medical procedures. But it doesn't look, sound, or feel medical to people who know you. There's no rash, high fever, broken bone, blood count, or anything concrete like that to confirm what you're telling them. Your screwed-up brain chemistry is invisible to the naked eye. And people who know you have maybe been thinking for a long time that you're just mean or crabby or unmotivated or irresponsible or in other ways "difficult." Educating them, patiently, will be an ongoing process and take repeat efforts.

- *Accept the possibility that the people in your life will rearrange themselves in ways that you don't anticipate and that hurts your feelings.*

In my case, some I thought would be right there for me were the first ones to run like hell, and some I thought would run like hell are still here right next to me. You can't blame the people who run like hell; mental illness is hard for people to understand, and we are afraid of what we do not understand. Not everyone will get it, and that's all right. If you can change or influence one mind for the better, that's a good thing. One mind at a time, that's what it's all about.

But, as my friend said, sometimes "people start coming out of the woodwork." When you remove your worry and obsessing

(*I wonder if they know*) from the picture, life often gets so much nicer. It never fails to amaze me how many people know someone with bipolar disorder or have the illness themselves, and are willing to share their experiences with me.

Should You Tell Your Boss?

A while back, I contacted a PR person with the thought of possibly hiring her to aid my career. She went to my website and checked out what I do. Then she sent me an email saying she'd decided not to work with me, because she believed that being treated with medication for mental problems was a sign of "weakness." That was her word. Was her reaction unusual? Not at all. When people in the work world know you have a mental illness, that knowledge can color their judgment of what you do and what you are capable of, whether they realize it or not or admit it or not.

So this is a big question: Should you tell your boss you're sick? And if you do, should you name it bipolar disorder or say you have "a thyroid problem"?

Again, there's no easy answer. Please be sure to think this one over very carefully. Remember, once it comes out of your mouth, it's not going back in and you can never make it disappear. To state the obvious: we rely on our jobs to support our families and, maybe, provide our health insurance, so caution and careful thought are in order. If you do tell, keep in mind that since most people do not understand anything about mental illness, the person or persons hearing your news may freak a little. Be prepared, and understand—more seriously—that disclosure may very well change your life on the job. I've heard from many bipolar individuals who believe they were passed over for job opportunities because their employers had a little less confidence in them than they did before they knew.

As you're thinking out carefully whether or not to tell the boss, consider a few questions:

Do you know what the law says about whether or not your employer must know if you're mentally ill?

The law has a lot to say; in fact, much of it is explained in the Americans with Disabilities Act. This is a federal act that spells out the requirements for private employers (with at least fifteen workers), state and local government workplaces, unions, and others. It's designed to protect you in various ways and at various stages of employment, including when you're applying for a job; getting hired; getting promoted; getting raises, benefits, and training; getting fired, and so on. Basically, you do not have to reveal your illness.

If you are interviewing for a new job, this prospective employer, during the job application process, might ask if you get along well with people, if you regularly get to work on time, stuff like that. He's not allowed to ask, "Are you now or have you ever been mentally ill?" So you might want to keep the words "bipolar disorder" out of the discussion. You are not required to tell him about this or any other illness you may have.

Will you need or do you want your employer to provide certain allowances for you because of your illness?

You got the job. But still, you have to see your doctor regularly for blood tests and you need an afternoon off once a month. Or you've been working for a while and your boss now wants to change your hours from the morning to the 3 to 11 p.m. shift, and you finally got yourself on a stabilized sleep rhythm, which this switch will mess up. Or you know you'd work better if your office or work station were in a quieter section.

If you want your employer to provide what are called "reasonable accommodations" (see the box on page 186 for the general categories of what those include), you will have to tell him why—and you probably can't get away with the "thyroid condition" explanation. The boss has a right to know, or rather, he is not required to make any of those adjustments for you unless you explain why you need them. He's entitled to ask you for specifics and, more to the point, maybe even require documentation of your medical situation.

But he must keep that information confidential. That might present the boss with some difficulties he doesn't especially want to face. He has obligations to a lot of other people. He's thinking, "If I'm gonna give this guy time off, let him come in late, change shifts, my other workers are going to resent that. But they don't know why I'm doing it. Looks like favoritism, bending the rules for one person, not for them. I don't need this grief." Just bear these issues in mind as you are weighing the pros and cons of coming out of your bipolar closet. I have met quite a few bipolars who reveal nothing, choosing even to pay for all their doctor appointments and treatments themselves rather than going through company health insurance.

A side note: If you have reason to think you've been discriminated against because of your illness or you're not being given the accommodations you need, be very, very careful before making a lot of noise. More than a few sick people are quick to jump on the old "I've got rights" bandwagon. Yes and no. What we have, good old bipolar disorder, is officially called a "mental impairment," and that is considered a disability. However, to get protection under the Americans with Disabilities Act, somebody has to decide your condition "substantially limits one or more major life activities"—such as, you can't see, hear, walk, care for yourself, or a number of other things. If you say, "You bet I've got a disability," and your boss says, "I don't think so," you can take the whole disagreement to court or complain to the Equal Employment Opportunity Commission. And you will likely open a can of worms with no guarantee of satisfaction. It's tough to convince an impartial observer that your invisible illness is disabling you, while at the same time you're perfectly capable of holding down your job or deserving of a promotion. In this situation—or if you're sure you got fired because you're bipolar—you need some good legal advice before taking action.

On a personal note, I would like to say that I do not now, nor will I ever, advocate suing a company for money, as I think this is what is wrong with America in general. If you need to take action, it should be only for your rights, not cash. Cash will change nothing. Suing for money will not change the stigma, it will only increase it. I am on the side of the employer: if you choose not to tell them about your illness, and then decide you need to be accommodated for something they did not know about, you should be fired for lying or hiding something. Sorry, mental health advocates: employers have rights, too, and it is not right to hide something and then expect them to change their company policies for you. This is a double-edged sword.

Is your employer tolerant, empathetic, and supportive, or the opposite?

Or here's another way of putting it: Do you work in a small, understanding, paternal/maternal place or do you work for a huge corporation with many levels of command that have something to say about you and your job? Do you have one boss to answer to, or are you in a place with department heads and assistant depart-

---

Reasonable Accommodations: What Might Help You on the Job, and What You Might Be Entitled To

You can request these changes to your work life if you need them or you believe they will help you be a happier, healthier, more effective employee. These are the kinds of adjustments the Americans with Disabilities Act spells out, what employers should provide.

- More flexible hours
- Self-paced workloads, or restructuring your job in similar ways
- Paid or unpaid leave if you have to be hospitalized
- A supportive supervisor
- Time off to see your doctor or psychiatrist
- Guidance and feedback about your job performance

Whether you decide to *ask* for any of this has a lot to do with the nature of your workplace, the kind of boss you have, how badly or well things are going on the job, and other highly individual factors. You should just know that these requests are officially sanctioned.

For complete information about your rights in the workplace, check out the website www.usdoj.gov/ctr/ada/adahom1.htm.

---

ment heads and assistant assistants, plus those things called human resources, personnel, or whatever? Neither situation is good or bad per se, but just know what and whom you will be dealing with if you tell them about your disorder.

Blessedly, I have escaped the need to work for a huge corporation with a hierarchical setup that would require me to be nice to a bunch of individuals I probably wouldn't like all that much. That's just me. Also blessedly, I have at times worked for people who trusted their instincts enough, and who were educated enough, to bend the rules and take their chances with me. Like Mike and Jim, the owner and VP of operations respectively of one of the largest car dealerships in my area. They knew I was not good at playing well with others, which they figured out early on when I announced that I wouldn't be following the dress code but would show up in jeans, cowboy boots, and polo shirts. "Fine," they said, "just sell cars." They found that despite, or because of, my creative brain and my unusual work habits I would deliver the product and services they needed. A couple of guys who were not only wildly successful businessmen, but men of character, compassion, and humanity. They saw me through some tough times, helped me get my confidence back, and they're still my friends.

In any case, what I *have* learned from talking to a lot of my fellow bipolars who do work in huge corporations is that it's smart and self-protective to do a little reconnaissance before you go and ask somebody to make allowances related to mental illness. The box on page 192 gives a brief description of some services that might be available to you. This is the "official line," so to speak. But, of course, these services are staffed by people, and some people are going to be better, more professional, more helpful, more empa-thetic than others. Know whom you will be dealing with.

"A good thing to do is to ask around among some of your coworkers, ones you trust, about what they've experienced or heard," says Annie, thirty-eight, who worked in the marketing department of a large organization in the hotel industry. Her office, she says, was "very political; everybody was always looking over their shoulder. So it was not too relaxed to start with. A few months ago, I was assigned a new supervisor, and we were like oil and water. She was dangerous to my health, literally. I felt myself starting to cycle into depression, very bad. There was another department I was pretty sure I could move into, so I wanted to talk to somebody about getting a transfer."

She asked around, very discreetly. "One man had been with the company a long time, and I noticed a lot of people sought him out for advice. He just had a great reputation as an honest person, trustworthy, someone who would tell you a straight story. I also had a good pal there who I knew had been to human resources recently about some issues she was having. What I heard from these two people wasn't very encouraging. Basically, they said you couldn't have a confidential conversation with HR, you couldn't expect much, they supported management more than you, and you might be asking for trouble to go to them."

Annie decided to bide her time, head off a serious depressive episode through some smart self-regulation techniques she knew worked well for her, while she quietly and actively looked for a job in another company. Which she found.

What's the culture of the organization you work for? What

might you anticipate from the people who have the power to influence your job? Do some groundwork on these questions before entering the lion's den.

I will get on my soapbox here and just send a message to any employers out there who happen to be reading this book. If you know that one of your best people—that reliable individual sitting at his or her desk or workstation or out on the packaging line—has started slipping, doesn't it make more sense for you to try to help him or her than to just cut that person loose? Or pass him or her up for a promotion or project? Isn't it better to know that you have a worker who is willing to share the information about bipolar disorder and request support, than to have one who is hiding it and maybe being less productive and confident on the job due to fear of exposure? If you, Mr. or Ms. Employer, have brought in experts to give your workers peppy talks about healthful eating, physical fitness, or the dangers of smoking, would you consider having someone come in to speak about staying mentally healthy? Just a thought.

Can you get the kind of help you need at work?

Everything I've said so far seems to be suggesting that keeping quiet, staying under the radar, and not telling the boss what's wrong with you is the safer course on the job. But not necessarily.

Thinking about the worst-case/best-case possible outcomes of disclosing your bipolar state of mind, you might conclude that possibly you can get some needed support from your employer if the company knows what you're up against. Some organizations are more evolved, enlightened, and educated about mental illness than others. Some organizations might be extremely helpful, maybe not out of the goodness of their heart, but because they want to hold on to an employee they value, someone who's making money for them. Justin, a man in his mid-thirties, is an example. He works as a designer for a large catering and event planning company. A highly creative guy, with a thousand brilliant ideas a minute, Justin also had a lot of trouble "keeping it all together," he says.

"I had a couple of other jobs before this one, and they both followed the same pattern. I start off great, everybody loves me, I'm feeling pumped and enthusiastic. My little touch of hypomania is doing just fine for me. Then I start going over the top, my output is inconsistent, I'm missing deadlines, everybody isn't loving me so much anymore. I blew it on those jobs. I really wanted to hold on to this spot, but I saw myself falling into that same pattern."

His problems at work, Justin relates, included not getting back to clients in a timely manner, arriving late for meetings, getting impatient with the "morons" at the meetings because he thought he had better ideas, going off in his own head and not reacting to what people were saying, losing track of stuff in his office, and starting down tangents that interested him but weren't on assignment. Justin's performance was becoming so erratic, and so annoying to others, that his boss had a talk with him.

"My boss is really a terrific guy. He told me he appreciated my efforts, that I'd made some real contributions, that he admired my creative spark. And he also pointed out my latenesses, all that other stuff, said I needed to improve in those areas, and what could he do to help me stay on track. Because he gave me that vote of confidence—and also I'd been there for over a year; I knew him and what kind of person he was—I told him about my bipolar disorder and the tendency to cycle into slightly manic behavior. Some good things came out of this talk. The man was true to his word. He helped me."

Among the good things that happened for Justin:

He and his boss agreed that Justin would probably benefit, and stay on track, with more one-on-one contact between the two of them. "I wasn't too crazy about this at first," Justin said, "because I like to work independently. But just having to give him regular updates turned out to be good for me. I needed that kind of imposed schedule."

The boss also arranged for Justin to have a number of sessions with a job coach, a professional who met with Justin and helped him figure out some ways he could better fit into the environment. "We talked about situations that typically bugged me," he said, "or situations where I was bugging somebody else, and she gave me some ideas on how to grease the wheels a little. Express myself in a better way. A little behavior modification, I guess you'd call it. Also, she helped me organize my workspace, which made an enormous difference."

So the moral of Justin's story might be, if you're someone that everybody loves—that is, the boss knows you've got a lot to offer, the organization values you—but bipolar is affecting your work and you're starting to mess up, or you really are going to need some time off, disclose your illness. You might get useful help. Take the lay of the land, give some thought to what these people are like, what you contribute to the business, and what would aid your healing. Not all huge corporations are evil empires.

Support Services in the Workplace

Many large companies have departments that exist for the purpose of seeing that employees are happy (mostly), employers are happy (mostly), people have a place to air their questions or requests or specific grievances, everybody understands the rules and regulations of the organization, and support services are available. Here, briefly, is what they are, what they do, and how they might be useful to you.

Human resources

This might be called the personnel department or employee relations or some other name. It might be composed of one person or a whole lot of people. Among other things, they're supposed to be of help to an employee who wants a transfer within the company, who feels he's been discriminated against, or who's having interpersonal problems on the job that he hasn't been able to fix on his own. Typically, you call and make an appointment to talk. You can ask if your conversation will be kept confidential, such as from your boss. If the HR person won't guarantee that, think about whether you want to go down this route at all.

People who have gone to HR for advice or support say it's important to know exactly what you're asking for and what you hope to accomplish; this isn't a place to complain or bemoan the unfairness of your life at work.

Employee assistance program

This might be called an employee hotline. Most big companies have such a service. The people who work in employee assistance programs, who might be outside professionals hired by the company, deal with mental health issues, which can include family problems and substance abuse. They're often psychologists or social workers, and they're expected to offer support to an employee who's feeling pressured or stressed or who's worried about his performance on the job. They can make recommendations for short-term counseling, disability leave, and the like. Generally, you can set up a meeting without the boss knowing about it.

Coaching

If you're a valued employee with smarts and talent, but you have some problems getting along with people or getting yourself organized, a job coach could help. This person might be a psychologist, and you might have a couple of sessions or meet every so often over several months. A coach can be a good person to serve as a kind of middleman between an employee and the boss, figuring out what accommodations the worker needs and explaining them to management. Some companies provide coaching as a job benefit. You can also hire one privately, and pay for it yourself. Do an Internet search for coaches.

There's also coaching or counseling through state services, typically called a department or division of vocational rehabilitation. You don't usually have to pay for this kind of help, which might involve finding out what kind of work would best suit your bipolar needs and what you can do to locate such jobs.

Should You Tell Your Coworkers?

A couple of questions to consider:

Are these people, the folks with whom you spend eight or more hours a day, friendly and supportive? Or are you toiling away in a dog-eat-dog, cutthroat, highly competitive environment, in which some one or some others will fall on any news of your illness as a possible boon for themselves?

Another question: How crazy have you been on the job?

Or, how much interpersonal damage have you left in your

manic-depressive wake? The fallout from a manic episode, especially, can have a long life span with workplace relationships. According to some studies, as much as five years later you may still be looked at as peculiar, even though you have yourself under control and haven't done anything too nutty in a long time.

My "reasons to tell / reasons not to tell" exercise can be informative. If you do tell a coworker or coworkers, you should be clear in your mind what you hope to accomplish or get from your disclosure. Generally, that falls under a few categories.

Because You Want to Apologize

If you've been inexcusably irritable, hostile, moody, or "high maintenance," you'll want to say you're sorry or at least offer an explanation. I have more to say on this score in a later chapter, on "making peace with the past," because most of us have probably acted at times like total creeps to people in our lives and it's a decent thing to do to tell those folks we're sorry. But in a workplace environment, you're not entitled to expect coworkers or colleagues to cut you a lot of slack. Aside from an apology being a decent thing to do, if you gave someone a hard time and you have to keep working with that someone, you'd better mend some fences.

One woman who had serious problems with depression before she got stabilized shared a small office with another woman during a difficult half year. "I was a total bitch to this very nice person who had the misfortune of having to work next to me," she said. "At the time, it took all my energy just to get my job done. I didn't want to talk to her, I didn't want her to talk to me, I was rude. It had to have been really unpleasant for her to come to work in the morning." She took her former office mate, who had moved to another part of the company, out for coffee one day and explained what had been wrong and how much she regretted her behavior.

Because You Want to Clear the Air or Set the Record Straight

Many bipolars say they detect a level of awkwardness among people they work with, uneasiness, maybe gossip, maybe guarded references. "I had to leave the office regularly for checkups, and I'd tell the person at the front desk that I had a doctor's appointment," said one woman. "This happened such a lot that I began to realize people were speculating about what was wrong with me. One day a woman I work with came over, just oozing with fake concern, and said that she knew I 'had some problems' and could she be of any help. I know this lady and I know she was fishing for information. It occurred to me that my saying nothing was fueling all kinds of talk around the place."

She mentioned casually to a friendly coworker why she needed regular doctor appointments, "and I figured, correctly, that news would get around and stop the speculation. This friend said to me, 'Oh, some people thought you were probably going for fertility treatments. They felt sorry for you that you couldn't have a baby.' I think mood disorder turned out to be a lot less juicy, because in a little while I wasn't picking up that gossipy vibe anymore."

Because You Want Practical Support

Maybe you need people to cover for you when you have to be out, to absorb some of your workload temporarily. You want them on your side.

"There are times when our work gets all of a sudden really heavy," said a man who's a computer specialist in a film production company connected to the advertising industry. "Fourteen-hour days, everybody's expected to put in overtime for a month, and that's just something I can't handle. The boss understands this. He's exempted me from those requirements, but the other people in my office don't know why, and there's been resentment. Once I told the guys I work with that I was bipolar and I had to stick to a schedule, and I said I really appreciated their understanding and support, things got a lot better. It helped that I let them know I was missing out on overtime pay!"

Because You Want Emotional Support

It can be tough to feel you're living a double life: off the job, friends and family are aware of all you do to keep your moods in check and to follow a careful medication and lifestyle routine; on the job, you're the sanest guy who ever lived, steady, stable, responsible—or at least, you're trying to act that way, and as the man said earlier, it's an enormous effort to maintain the front.

Most of us do strike up a friendship or two with a coworker or feel close to someone we maybe don't know all that well but sense is a good egg and a kind human being. You are spending, probably, one-third of your waking hours on the job. That's a lot of your life. Maybe you'll feel better, not so split in two, to know that someone there knows, and cares, and wishes the best for you. A little emotional support never hurt anybody.

Whatever your "reasons to tell," a few suggestions:

Don't belabor the whole thing. This is a piece of information about yourself that you want your coworker to be aware of, and he or she doesn't need to hear a lot of background about research into mental illness, why it's no longer called manic depression, and all that.

Don't recount your most hideous excesses of the past in an attempt to "prove" that you really were sick and you're better now. I am all in favor of sharing our bipolar stories, as you know, but this is not the audience to do that with. Keep the gory details for your support group.

Tell once, not twice. Once the cat is out of the bag, so to speak, you don't want to be dropping the words "bipolar disorder" into casual conversations around the copying machine. Let it go.

Kids: What They Can and Can't Understand about a Bipolar Parent or Relative

"When are you coming home, Daddy?" Those are the words I heard so many times over the phone, when I was off on one of my flash-in-the-pan manic trips or coming out of a drunken funk in some hotel room and I called my family. More often than not, I'd been having a conversation, of sorts, with my wife, she pleading with me to get home, get some sleep, me ignoring her pleas, until finally, Lisa—disgusted, tired, emotionally torn apart—would say quietly, "Do you want to tell the kids good night?" So one by one they'd get on the phone.

"Hey, Winkie, how was school?" I'd ask. Winkie is my nickname for my older daughter.

"Fine."

"What did you learn today?"

"Nothing." This was her typical answer, which she thought was the funniest joke in the world and always set her off laughing hysterically. I'd ask her to put Alex, her brother, on the phone.

"Okay, Daddy," Winkie would say. "When are you coming home?"

"Soon, honey, soon."

"ALEX!" she'd yell. Why is that? Why do kids always yell in the phone?

Alex would get on.

"Hey, Alex, how's it going, pal?"

He would tell me a little about his day, the math test he just had.

"Okay, son, I love you."

"I love you, too, Daddy. Hey, Daddy, when are you coming home?"

"Probably on Friday, buddy, I have a few things to do first. . . ."

Always those words: When would I be home? When would they see me again? It's still painful to remember how often my kids had to ask me that. It still makes me want to cry when I think of the time I wasted because my brain was broken. Because I didn't get help so much sooner than I did. I missed so much.

Once I was diagnosed, we pretty much sat our two older kids down and let them in on what was going on. They were nine and ten; our youngest was only age three and not yet ready for the whole story. I told them the doctor had told me that I had a mental illness, called bipolar disorder, and in fact I was extremely glad to learn that I was sick and not just crazy. I told them this explained why sometimes I'd been running around like a chicken without a head and sometimes closing myself in my room and not talking to anybody, among other weird behaviors. I told them I wasn't going to die from this illness, I would be taking pills to help me get better, but it was probably going to be hard to find the right kind of pills for my body. And during that hard road, I added, I might very well still go lock myself in my room sometimes—this, of course, would be the same-old, same-old for them.

We faced the whole thing together, and within a matter of days the kids were going online and printing out articles for me to read about the illness. So they've been in on the recovery with me. We hide nothing, and they have access to everything. As they have questions or concerns, they ask and we address them. If something is about to happen, I let them know, I keep them posted. If my medication stops working and I have to adjust, I let them know. We tell them if I'm having a bad day and they stay clear. Recently, having one of those bad days, I came home from the office and went right to my safe place, the comfy chair in my bedroom, telling my kids I would be out for the night, I needed a little quiet and space. They understood. I think they appreciate this kind of openness a whole lot more than the days when I was just a miserable SOB to be around. And I like to think that the experience has helped them to learn it's always smart to educate themselves and to seek help when they need it.

Children, I believe strongly, need and want to be told and taught about life, including the part about how it's filled at times with disappointment, sorrow, and even illness. Children, I also believe, can generally understand a hell of a lot more and handle a hell of a lot more than we give them credit for. But they can't understand what you hide from them, obviously, even if you're doing it in the guise of protecting them. Difficulties come, sooner or later; prepare them with the truth.

Let your children in. Share with them what they need to hear about this illness, and nine times out of ten, those kids will become closer to you and your recovery process. Very often, kids accept the information with a flood of relief: *Dad/Mom was acting that way because he/she was sick, not because he/she was mad at me or I did something wrong.*

Disclosure, at the same time, has to be tempered by the kind of relationship you have with your children or their ages or your marital strains or all manner of other real-life factors. Bipolar disorder isn't happening in a vacuum.

Maryann is a single mother raising a fourteen-year-old daughter, Amanda. "It has been no picnic for this kid living with her crazy mother," says Maryann, forty. "I used to do some dumb, dumb things, got involved with a couple of men, got dumped, sunk into terrible depressions. From time to time, I sent Amanda to live with my mother for a while, and fortunately, my mom was always willing and a terrific grandma.

"When I got on good medication a year ago and I knew what was wrong with me, I told Amanda all about it, but she didn't really want to hear too much. Every now and then, I'll say something about bipolar, and she says, 'Mom, drop it, okay?' I thought about this reaction, and I chalk it up to a few things. She's a teenager, she's into her friends and her life and she doesn't want a whole song and dance from me. Maybe she's just kind of a squeamish kid, like once I was talking about breast-feeding her as a baby and she gave me a disgusted look and left the room. Too much information.

"And mainly, maybe, she doesn't know if she can entirely trust me. Is old Mom going to go around the bend again and start acting crazy? Maybe she's angry at me for what used to happen. So I've got to build up that trust gradually. And I'll ask her if she wants to talk about anything that happened and about what I'm doing now. I'm trying to be more sensitive to what she might be feeling."

With very young kids, you're probably not going to come out with the words "I have a mental illness." First of all, they don't know what that means exactly, and second, "illness" is scary: *Mom is sick, maybe she's going to die.* They don't know what "manic" means or what "depression" means. Parents with young children say they have good results tying any explanation into experiences or times the kids will clearly remember:

"You know how Mom gets so grouchy sometimes and just wants to stay in bed and she doesn't want you to talk to her? Well, I found out why I get that way, and now I'm taking some medicine that will make me better."

Don't Tell, Show

I've been talking here about what to say to people, and when and
why. Just as important, in fact more so, is what you do. What you
learn is that actions speak loudly. So I educate in part by the way
I handle my life and my actions. Gone are the days of being able
to fly off the handle at someone who makes me angry—as many
"normal" people are allowed to do—because then the reaction is,
"Oh, Bipolar Guy is going postal again," and the message is, anyone with bipolar illness is a weird dude who can't control his
aggression and should be avoided. So while it isn't always easy, I
choose to educate by trying—*trying*—to always keep my mind in
focus and not lose control.

One group of people I meet in my talks I think of as the "consumers," people with bipolar disorder. When I speak to an audience
of consumers, it is fun, sad, aggravating, emotional, but mostly,
rewarding as hell. They are there, I think, for three reasons: to get
confirmation of the fact that they can get better, to hear things that
make them feel not alone, and to see if there's something they are
missing. They hope to spot a little light at the end of the tunnel and
to validate their feelings or their methods of dealing with this illness. My approach with other nutty people like me is to be in your
face, balls to the wall, hold nothing back. I don't have to hold anything back, because they've seen it, they feel it, they know it.

So maybe this is a form of educating, too, providing a sense of
community and a sense of hope. And my audience of "consumers"
is providing me with the same thing. Every time I speak I learn

something new, and that's partly because I don't just speak, I listen. I listen to what they say and how they react, and I watch their eyes for my own validation.

Listen to others who are positive, active in their treatment, getting control of the fox. Let yourself be educated by them. It is so nice not to be alone in this world.

NINE

"I Burned a Lot of Bridges"

Making Peace with Your Past and Repairing Damage

You cannot live in the past and you cannot beat yourself up endlessly over the things that you have done—and without doubt, you've done a barrelful of weird, wacky, hurtful, damaging things. And you are probably left now with a barrelful of rotten feelings—of regret, guilt, embarrassment, shame, and anger, too. In my case, I've had to deal with the fallout from twenty-some years of acting like a nut. In particular, the three leading up to my diagnosis and beginning treatment were filled with enough drama, problems, scandal, and other really cool stuff to make a great movie, with one loathsome character charging through the plot.

When I mention this topic, making peace with your past, bipolar people know right away what I'm talking about. They nod their heads. "Hey, when you're manic and you're sailing above all the pathetic, ordinary fools in the world," said one woman, "you don't think twice about telling somebody where they can stick it." Another, who barely survived crazy buying sprees and dragged her husband into deep debt, said, "You know as you're plopping down that credit card that you shouldn't be, but you don't care. Because you believe, you're absolutely convinced, that you will replace that money before the charge even clears the bank. Yes indeed, your ship is gonna come in, big time."

The toughest peace to reach for involves the people you've treated badly. Lord knows, I burned a lot of personal bridges. And I mean World War II amounts of bridges, and unlike the U.S. Army, when I blew one up there was nothing much left but a hole. Actually, I have no clear idea of how many of them I set in flames, because I am still missing collectively about five years of my life, five years that I cannot seem to remember. Maybe it was the illness, maybe it was the drinking, maybe it's just a blur now because I want it to be. Regrettably, the number of bridges seems to grow as I run into more people from the old days. "Oh, I told you to go screw yourself, did I? When you were just trying to give me a break and a helping hand? Sorry, I don't remember that, but I apologize anyway."

But the bigger question is: what has become of the fires I set since treatment and recovery? I consider that a hugely important part of this book; most people with bipolar disorder, according to what I hear from my audiences, are either getting better or staying sick, by which I mean not truly moving into the light of a stabilized bipolar life, precisely because of the way they deal with the past. The past, after all, can stop anyone in their tracks, sick or not.

When the past is littered with the fallout of our rages and depressions, bizarre behaviors, and suicidal threats or actions, that's a landscape that's doubly, triply hard to look back at and clean up.

Guilt, fear, and downright shame make it difficult to have any positive thoughts about ourselves and our future. When you review the mistakes associated with your illness, it's easy to reach a point at which you will not allow yourself to recover from them. You spend a lot of time walking with your head down. But you need to get your head up as far as possible, in order to see what's in front of you. Avoid beating yourself up over the mistakes, definitely, but acknowledge them. That, my friends, is what will help you get better. Face the music, change the station a tad, and keep moving on.

So I want to offer here a few "rules," let's call them, for making peace with the past, and they fall into two rough categories: one, where and as best as you can, patch up the old damages of yesterday; two, develop a new, better mindset for today. Without getting too philosophical about it, I'll just add this thought: What we need to do in order to reach a level of success in controlling bipolar disorder is pretty much what all people, including those who are not mentally ill, need to do in order to succeed in life in general.

Make the Hard Phone Calls

Get in touch with the people you blew off or avoided in the bad days. We've all done it, all of us. After speaking to thousands of people who are battling bipolar disorder, I can accurately say that every single one has cut someone off. And every single one isn't entirely sure why he or she did that.

Here's one common reason, I believe. Many of us in "club bipolar" are helpers. We're there for others when they're in some difficulty, ready to do whatever has to be done. When it comes to ourselves, however, accepting help is something we will not allow to happen. The strong, self-sufficient people with this illness do not want anyone to see them in a needy position. In my own case, I know this peculiar characteristic probably accounts for a large share of the problems I created for myself over the years. "Yeah, I'm in real bad shape, I'm desperate, but I don't want you to see me like this, go away!" Then my concerned friend or relative would go away, and I'd be furious. Where did everybody go? How come no one is here for me?!

Sounds familiar?

Not only did I push away my wife and kids, I cut off all communication with two of my best friends in the world, my cousin and my pal from high school days. I stopped taking their calls, stopped going out with them, just dropped the whole contact. Maybe I'd make a quick call every now and then, empty promises to get together and "do something." Except I was lying every time, because I knew I could not and would not. They'd say, "How are things going?" and I'd say, "Great," and I hated the lie. It was just easier to steer clear of them. I realize now that I could not stand having these guys see me as I had become—weak, as I thought of myself then. Didn't want them to see that I was out of control and could not manage to get my mind straight.

Reaching out to the good people you shut out in the past is

hard to do. You may miss those people or those possibilities, you value them, you would like to recover them and recoup your losses, if at all possible. On the one hand, you now feel worthy of those relationships. On the other hand, and this is the kicker, you still may not have forgiven yourself for the way you behaved. You are stuck in that frame of mind that says, *God, I was such an ass to them back then, how can I talk to them now? What do I say?*

Just pick up the phone, tell your story, see what happens. It's part of healing to give it a try, and I do know this: You get better with every call you make. You discover that some of the burned bridges weren't gone for good, only closed for repair. With those two close friends, my cousin and my pal from high school, I have made the hard phone calls. I've said in so many words that I regret having tuned them out for so long. I've explained about my illness and what I am doing these days to control it. And they are back in my life, people I rely on and who rely on me. They actually never really left, but were waiting for me to get my act together and reach out. You probably have some folks like that in your life.

Don't Expect to Be Forgiven

Not everyone you treated badly is going to let bygones be bygones. Hope for forgiveness; don't expect it. And don't get mad if it is not forthcoming.

We set out to repair. We approach the person we hurt or blew off. We describe a little of what life was like for us at the time, we say we regret those behaviors, we're sorry for a particular way we acted or for something we said. So far so good. But then, what can so easily happen: We get a little testy when we don't receive that guy's blessing in return. Or if not testy, we're hurt. Maybe pissed.

Karen, a thirty-five-year-old social worker, experienced extreme manic episodes throughout her mid and late twenties. Many of them, she said, included "little salvation missions I went on among people I knew. I 'saw' what was wrong with everybody else and I knew how they needed to fix it. There was one friend I saw a lot of during that time, and I decided I was going to save her from herself. I initiated astonishing conversations with her, doing this I believed totally out of the goodness and the wisdom of my heart, because I had heightened insights, I had religion, I had the meaning of life. Some of these talks I realized later were so offensive, so insulting. 'Sally,' I'd say, 'I sense that you are carrying around so much anger, I want you to meditate with me,' stuff like that. I showed up at her apartment around seven in the morning one Saturday and I told her to put on her coat, I was taking her to an AA meeting because she needed to admit that she was an alcoholic. Actually, Sally was doing just fine, I had no reason to think she was an alcoholic. As for any anger, that was probably directed at me."

The friend made herself increasingly unavailable. When Karen finally got her moods stabilized, she reached out to Sally again.

"I wanted to hear her say something like, 'Oh, that's okay, forget about it, it's all water under the bridge.' Or maybe, 'You were never as impossible as all that, what are you talking about? No problem.' I didn't hear any of that. She was actually pretty cool to me and she didn't suggest we meet for coffee or anything, and that felt like a rejection. Well, it was a rejection. So I'm thinking this over, and what I'm realizing is that I was making it all about me. I wanted to get something specific back that would make me feel better. And I was ignoring the possibility that my bad behavior maybe wasn't going to be so easily whitewashed away."

Two or three rights do not make up for a wrong. So extend your apology. Offer your regrets. Explain your behavior to the extent you want to. Hope for understanding and a fresh start. But it's a mistake, I believe, or maybe pushing your luck to expect to be forgiven for all your past sins.

Professional Damages Are Extremely Hard to Repair

When your past weird, hurtful, or damaging behaviors involved work colleagues or associates, you have at best a fifty-fifty chance of recouping your losses. This isn't about the caring friends you blew off. This is about the people you crossed swords with or badly let down within work situations, and who may not be too interested in your explanations now. Getting back in anyone's good graces, if it happens at all, takes patience, determination, and a steady demonstration of "sanity" over time.

A bipolar friend described to me a period, about ten years ago, when he hit his personal rock bottom. Lewis was then, and is now, a salesman in the health care field. Back then, he was maintaining his job, while the rest of his life crumbled around him.

"I found myself homeless in February on a Sunday night. I

spent this evening sitting in a Baptist church, hung over, listening to everyone scream 'Save me, Jesus.' I was looking at my pregnant girlfriend, whose child was not mine. I was way far gone.

"I got back to my car, crawled inside, and nearly froze to death. Drove to work in the morning. I decided the car was not the best place to get my beauty sleep, so the next night I hid out in a storage area at work after closing and slept there. Then I started hanging out after closing in the VP's suite, where there was a bathroom, shower, kind of my own Holiday Inn. I lived there for six months, eating my dinners from the snack machine in the hallway. Everyone at the job remarked how I always got to work early.

"One night I woke up to voices, not the ones in my head, but somebody's conversation. I realized it wasn't night, but midmorning. I'd overslept, and I was hearing our VP on a conference call in the outside room. I cleaned myself up, then waited him out for an hour, trying to time my exit to when he answered another call. But when I slipped out he stopped me with a hand signal. I had to explain myself, one of the most humiliating moments of my life. He told me he was 'disappointed' to hear how I'd been living there, and told me he had to let me go so I could 'get off the merry-go-round' I was obviously on."

That's what Lewis chose to do—get off the merry-go-round. He took the necessary actions to regain his well-being, by starting and sticking with a treatment program and staying sober. At rock bottom, Lewis was a man who lost his family, his dignity, most of his money, and more, and yet he was able to put his professional life back together. That didn't happen easily and it didn't happen quickly. "I asked to have the opportunity to prove myself," he said, "I asked for a second chance. And I was grateful for that. Very gradually, I rebuilt my relationship with my boss, gained everyone's trust again. Occasionally, the topic of the old days pops up between us, and he smiles and says my honesty pulled me through. Honesty, yes. But also I worked harder than I ever had before. I became accountable for myself, no excuses. I had to deliver value to the company, and I demonstrated I could do that."

Every story will not have a happy or entirely satisfactory ending, of course. Sometimes a professional reputation takes a permanent hit from shooting-oneself-in-the-foot bipolar behaviors. Still, I think facing the music as best you can is good for your mental outlook, good for forgiving yourself and reclaiming a little more of your self esteem. Facing the music might involve extending a difficult apology, which is something I know about.

Given my nature and given my job as a comic entertainer, loaded onto bipolar disorder, it's probably not surprising that I went beyond merely burning bridges, if you'll bear with my little analogy some more. No, I got as much gasoline as I could, poured it on, and torched them. I was good at it. But again, I will not make the equation that I destroyed relationships and contacts because I was sick. I can say, however, that I was quick to light the fires because surely my judgment was a lot off at the time.

An example:

During a rather manic period, when I seemed to be doing well onstage in the comedy clubs, I was feeling higher than I should have and than I actually was. I had begun headlining at this point, around age twenty-eight or twenty-nine, being the main act onstage, so that was a big deal. Yet I was so damn angry, because alternating with the mania I was also enduring bouts of depression that I just could not seem to snap out of. I found myself feeling very lost, having a lot of trouble with the whole "the world is screwed up" thing. I'd do my show, head right back to the hotel room, get drunk, pass out. There was one problem: the Internet.

There was a community of comedians and club owners in several chat rooms, which were called something else then. The communication went on during the night, after the clubs closed and a bunch of jazzed-up comics wanted to swap stories. Wow, now I could log on and find people to fight with! I could go to the chat room of choice and make posts that would thoroughly piss people off. So I'd just whack the heck out of the person I had in my sights—attacks on his character and his appearance, disparagements of his talents, insults to his family, all expressed in the juiciest, rottenest language I had at my disposal.

As it happened, one of the individuals I was most ferociously whacking was a well-liked comic, a famous name. The fire started out a small blaze, then grew to pretty mammoth proportions as I in turn became the subject of attack by a lot of powerful people in the upper regions of the little comedy world. Of course, the more they went after me, the more I went after them. That's part of the mania, the distorted self-perception; right then, I felt as though I didn't need anyone, and so I pulled out all the stops. And I pretty much ended my comedy career right then and there. I was still able to get work occasionally, but it was a very long time before I realized the extent of the damage I'd done.

Fast-forward a few years: I was at a fund-raiser in California, and who walks into the club but the big-shot comic involved in

my little ruckus. I knew I had burned the bridge and it was probably not going to be rebuilt anytime soon, but I understood deep in
my bones that I had to at least approach the man and tell him I
was wrong to say the things I had said and that I regretted having
done so. I walked over, introduced myself (we hadn't met before,
though he sure knew my name), and spoke my piece. He extended
his hand, we shook, and that was about it. No, we were not going
to be cordial colleagues in the same crazy business, but that ugly
little chapter had been closed after a fashion.

Marking "closed" to a past work-related experience or period
of time that did you damage sometimes takes just making peace
with it all in your own mind, or in your heart. There may be no
one to explain things to or apologize to. A woman who pursued a
career in the publishing world said this: "In the magazine business, you often get ahead by moving from one magazine to
another at a higher job title. I worked as an editor at two national
women's magazines, and I was let go from both jobs because of
reviews that said my performance was 'erratic.' This was largely
because of disabling depressive episodes I went through before I
was finally successfully treated on medication. But I could not get
another job, even at a lower title. I called people I used to work
with and asked them for any leads or recommendations, and they
were polite and diplomatic, but clearly unwilling to be helpful.
That's a pretty insular world, really. There was a red flag next to
my name, and it was not going to go away."

She found a job in another field and has been content with
that. "But a big problem was getting over the bitterness and
resentment that I harbored for a long time. It was partly directed

at myself, for messing up. Mostly, it was directed at people I felt had just written me off." She's still working at getting over those feelings, she said, "by keeping my focus on the present, keeping my ego out of it. Business is business."

Often, the people you've crossed paths with in the work world have no reason to feel kindly disposed toward you—they don't love you, they don't particularly care for you one way or another, you're on a professional level. You may never recoup all your losses or entirely resurrect your reputation. Make peace with the fact, and it will help you get better.

Know When to Let the Past Fade Out

In an earlier chapter, I talked about how critical it is for a bipolar to stay away from the people who aren't so good for us—definitely avoid the hard-partying friend who wants you to go out barhopping or the guy who keeps telling you there's no such thing as mental illness. But in this matter of making peace with your past, you might come to realize that a relative, a close friend, someone who's been kind and caring, is also someone you just can't have in your new life—at least, for the time being. Maybe family history is so loaded with complications and ancient resentments that your self-preservation and recovery require you to let that part of the past go. I'm a big believer in trusting your gut instincts in many cases. If your instincts are saying that a clean slate, a fresh start, is necessary for your healing, maybe that's what you need, at least until you're feeling fairly well stabilized.

I think we should not—we *cannot*—judge each other and rate personal motivations or requirements on some absolute scale ("She was always nice to me during some bad, bad times, so I have to make it up to her now"). Life is not so tidy. Human psyches are more complex.

A woman who has been on a successful medication regimen for five years, doing well, told this story, an example of what I'm getting at. Angie is thirty-nine; her sister, Paula, is forty-eight. Angie has had no contact with her sister in over two years. She said:

"Paula and I share stuff that no one else could understand. You know that Tolstoy quote, that happy families are all alike but unhappy families are not alike because each one is unhappy in its own way. That's what she and I know, the ways in which our family was unhappy. Mother frustrated and angry, father drinking too much and angry. An old familiar story, but the devil is in the details, and Paula and I know the details.

"Partly because she was nine years older than me, she was my kind of substitute mother, my rock, and that was especially true when I went through years of depression, suicidal thoughts, then running around doing dangerous, stupid things. Throughout my twenties and early thirties, I was always messing up on jobs and going through one disastrous love affair after another. Paula let me live with her for stretches of time. She talked me down from nutty highs and up from horrible low points. She ran interference with our parents. She probably saved my life.

"I should be nothing but appreciative and grateful to her. Well, when I was finally diagnosed and on the medication and starting to feel like I could actually live sort of normally, I met a really nice guy and we got married. We moved out to Washington State, where he grew up, far away from my family in Hartford, and we opened a little business taking people out on fishing boats. I made a 180-degree turnaround in just about every aspect of my life, my home, my job, everything. Things are good. Over these past several years, Paula repeatedly reached out. She called, sent letters, packages, photos, emails. I rarely responded and I never reached out myself first, and finally a couple years ago, she just stopped. I guess she's given up on me.

"I'm not sure why I've acted this way. I've tried to analyze it. Maybe partly it's shame. I was such a mess and she knew it all. She's never said anything like that, but she's a reminder anyway. Maybe having her in my life today puts us back in the old positions. Me, the screwed-up mess who always needed to be bailed out, she the bailer. Me, the daughter who was a worry to our parents. When I used to talk to her, I got the feeling in some tiny ways that she sort of missed the old arrangement, she the rescuer and the good girl, and me the mess. And I can hardly blame her for that—the role she played for all those years must have been a big part of her life or her notions about herself.

"Yes, I am sad and regretful that I've cut off contact with her, but I'm happier and calmer since I've done so. I still think maybe someday we can be old ladies together and best friends. Maybe I just need more time."

Angie's story is not all that unusual. There can be a kind of major reshuffling of old relationship patterns that takes place when you start getting better. It might be a while before everybody gets on the same page. Or maybe that will never happen. You can't separate yourself from your history, but sometimes you have to tell yourself that that person, that relationship, has to stay in the past if you are to move forward. And it's not necessarily a destructive person, experience, or relationship, only one that it's too difficult to be around or to think much about.

We all make our peace in the way that works best.

Believe You Are a Deserving Human Being

This effort begins by acknowledging a tough truth: nothing, and I mean nothing, that you do or say now will make what you did before go away. Whatever your bad, nutty, hurtful behaviors back then were, they are pretty much there forever. We know that intellectually, we're not stupid, but a lot of those past experiences are captured in our minds in vivid Technicolor, and we keep replaying them. So I say, when that little videotape starts running again in your head and you're cringing at the sight, just try to turn it off. Flip the switch. It will only make you feel lousy about yourself.

Believe you are deserving.

I think I am safe in saying that probably 99 percent of the individuals who have this illness and who are going through a rough time are walking around thinking, *I don't deserve . . . my wife, my car, my job, my boss, my friends, my comfortable bed with the nice clean sheets . . .* whatever. But getting better is an ongoing process, like for the rest of your life, and it requires believing that you are just as deserving as anybody to *be* better and be healthy and live in the light.

A while back, a woman came up to me at the end of one of my talks about mental illness and said, "You have such an important message. How can I help you reach more people? What do you need?" She took out her checkbook. A second woman just behind her said, "I'd like to help, too." I said, "No, no, thank you, no." My thought was, *I don't deserve your help, I'm not worthy of it.* That happened to me more than once. Then I'd find myself back in my hotel room, praying, *God, why aren't you helping me do this work?*

I now realize that when I die and get up to the gate and say, *Hey, how come you didn't help me?* God will answer, *Well, how many women with checkbooks did you want me to send?* I've changed my thinking. I do want to reach more people with what I have to say, and I can't do it without some financial support, and I will accept it. I am deserving of help.

Try to Be a Better Person Today Than You Were Yesterday

Repair the way you feel about yourself as a human being by trying to be a better one right now.

I asked a bipolar friend of mine about this "making peace with the past" idea, and he said this: "We all have our little fatal flaws. They are flaws of character. One of mine is resorting to sarcasm when I'm not getting what I want or someone is acting like an idiot. I was a sarcastic asshole before I got on medication and I'm still a sarcastic asshole *on* medication. It's important to recognize ourselves as the total portrait, and not have all our tendencies viewed through the filter of bipolar disorder. However, my untreated bipolar years were hard on a lot of people, me most of all. I fight against a low opinion of myself, and one very valuable way to do that is by making a conscious effort to not act like a sarcastic asshole. That's a thing I can do something about. Sarcasm is the language of the devil, as someone once said."

My fatal character flaw—actually, one of quite a handful—is my tendency to become quickly and totally pissed at people. So what am I doing? I no longer get angry at the kid at McDonald's who messes up my order and forgets to put the fries in my bag, which I find out when I get home. Yes, it was his job to make sure the fries were in there, but packing up burgers at McDonald's is no picnic, poor kid. I might get a little annoyed at myself for not checking my order before I left the store. I might tell myself a box of fries is something I can do without anyway.

The clerk at my grocery store apologized for ringing up one of my items twice. I said, "If this is the worst thing that happens to me today, then I'm one lucky son of a gun and I should go out right away and buy a bunch of lottery tickets." That got more of a laugh than a lot of the jokes I used to tell onstage. The ticket agent at the airport finally punched me through, after a forty-five-minute wait on the random search line, and I said, "God bless, thanks a lot." The fellow looked and me and said, "Man, I wish we had more people like you coming through here."

This is the attitude I try to adopt, to be a better person than I used to be. The new, improved Paul Jones. It's actually not that hard. When you're in control of your bipolar disorder, you're likely to let a lot of things roll off you more easily than before. I know that I used to get upset at stuff that now I can honestly say holds little or no meaning for me. Not because those things don't matter or are totally unimportant, but because they pale in comparison to the darkness that I lived. Along the way, I like to think my new improved attitude spreads a little goodwill in the air we all breathe.

Embrace Your Spiritual Side

At the risk of sounding like a Bible thumper here, I want to address another major part of making peace with the past, and for me that is spirituality. I'm not talking about religion as such, and I'm certainly not talking about what's right for everyone. But there was a time, a long time, when I felt I was walking this planet without anyone or anything. I'm sure you're familiar with the feeling. Bipolar disorder is such a lonely illness.

It was not until I realized that instead of walking I was standing still, because I was keeping myself to myself, that I truly began to get better. One of the biggest steps for me was to allow myself to believe in something again. I believe there is a God, and God placed me on this earth for a reason, and most things happen for a reason. It's simple: for me, faith in something was way better than faith in nothing.

You can't live your life looking back. Drive your car with your head turned around peering out the rear window, and you'll crash.

But if you look back at your unregulated bipolar days in a thoughtful and constructive way, lose the self-blame and the guilt, take some good restorative actions, it pays off. For one thing, making peace can have the effect of proving to people who've been watching you warily out of the corners of their eyes for a long time that you've come down to earth, you're not nutty anymore. Or at least not as nutty as you used to be. It's more proof to your loved ones that you're determined to stay on a healthful track, you're serious about your recovery.

Maybe most important, making peace with the past amounts to "owning" your illness. It's real. It was there before and it's still there now, though your symptoms may be under control and you are in many ways a different person. We all need a clear-eyed acceptance of ourselves as individuals always living with a mental illness.

"A Blessing in a Really Big Disguise!"

A woman who has been living successfully with bipolar disorder for a number of years was reflecting on her many activities and accomplishments, which included running her own business as a designer and baker of ritzy wedding cakes, volunteering in several capacities in the AIDS community, and trekking in Nepal, "which seems to be the 'in' thing to do for a lot of women hitting fifty, like me. Today, I think that having bipolar disorder has been a blessing in disguise. A really, really big disguise, but nevertheless! I truly believe that I have insights and talents that are part and parcel of this condition. And the experiences I've gone through have made me a stronger person. Optimistic. Enthusiastic about life."

Her words hit me. She wasn't saying that being bipolar was something she reluctantly accepted, something she learned to put up with. She called it a blessing. I'm with her. I have said before and I'll probably say it a million more times before I die that I thank God for my illness. I really do. I consider myself extremely blessed that I've been given the opportunities and the lessons I have had, and many of those opportunities and lessons are because of my illness.

Bipolar disorder is directly linked to my creative side. It's what fueled my songwriting and my comedy career, and while that wasn't all great by any means, those experiences let me meet some really wonderful people. There is no feeling in the world better than having someone come up to you and give you a hug, shake your hand, and say, "I needed that laugh." That happened to me a lot over the years, and it makes you feel pretty damn good about yourself and even the pain you've been in. Not only did I help some of these great people, but they helped me as well.

Speaking to groups today about mental illness has given me exposure to an incredible number of individuals who feel the same way I do mentally, who have gone through a lot of the same stuff that I have, and many have been way more genuinely inspiring than I ever will be. Many of their stories have changed my life, just as much as mine may have influenced theirs.

Bipolar disorder has helped me to be more reflective and, I think, more caring at times than many people. It has allowed me to go so low as to be able to see today just how lucky I am not to be in that place anymore. It has shown me who my friends are and who they are not. It landed me in tough situations that I overcame, and that strengthened me. I have fallen down, blown up, made hundreds of thousands of dollars, lost it all, got it back and lost it again, all of which has taught me that no matter how bad it gets I will, in fact, survive.

It has made me appreciate my wife and my family beyond all measure.

Yes, indeed, a blessing in disguise.

I hope that some of the stories and suggestions I've shared in this book have encouraged you to view bipolar disorder not as a life sentence of doom, but as a very common illness that you can get under control and even, maybe, appreciate. Maybe come to love! The path from the dark into the light isn't an easy one to walk, but come along and join me on the journey.

RESOURCES

Bipolar Disorder, Depression, and Mental Illness Information

Paul Jones, Bipolar Boy (www.bipolarsurvivor.com and www.paulejones.com)
At my websites you will find: news you can use, like links to other sites of interest to those of us with bipolar disorder, and mental illness facts and updates; some inspirational stories from some inspirational folks; occasional scheduled online chats, when we can connect; fitness suggestions; and more. Please come visit. And come back again.

Depression and Bipolar Support Alliance (www.dbsalliance.org)
Formerly called the National Depressive and Manic-Depressive Association, this resource offers all kinds of help, from how to recognize the signs and symptoms to what it feels like and what to think about if you (or your loved one) has just been diagnosed. It also offers ways to get involved in mental health advocacy work. The alliance sponsors hundreds of support groups.

National Alliance on Mental Illness (www.nami.org)
I have been a speaker at NAMI meetings, and this is a great organization. Check out the site for news about research studies and clinical trials, fact sheets on a variety of mental health topics, discussions of public policy issues, local divisions you might want to join, publications you can order, and NAMI walks.

International Foundation for Research and Education on Depression
(www. ifred.org)
You will find the latest research on depression, and useful links to ways family and friends can be helpful and get some support for themselves.

Resources

Mental Health America (www.nmha.org)

This extensive site will link you to a variety of services and specific news, including medical updates on mental health issues, an events calendar of talks and conferences, and a crisis hotline.

Bipolar Disorders Treatment Information Center (www.miminc.org)

An excellent resource for information on mood stabilizers and all medications used in the treatment of bipolar disorder.

Depression and Related Affective Disorders Association (www.drada.org)

A Johns Hopkins–affiliated service, DRADA has information for self-help groups, newsletters you can receive, and updates about research programs. Under its umbrella you will find www.depressedteens.com, with links to many resources devoted to issues of adolescent depression.

Bipolar Significant Others (www.bpso.org)

This resource is designed for the support folks in the life of a bipolar relative or friend. Its members informally exchange ideas and information through a private Internet mailing list.

Mental Health News (www.mhnews.org)

Published by an individual who recovered from debilitating depression, this resource is intended "to fill the gap in community mental health information." Full of news about advocacy, treatment options, and community programs of interest.

American Mental Health Alliance (www.americanmentalhealth.com)

Useful advice on how to choose a therapist, how to locate one (by state listing), and the various kinds of psychotherapy available.

National Depression Screening Day (www.mentalhealthscreening.org)

A hugely important and valuable service, National Depression Screening Day was started about sixteen years ago. It's organized through local clinics, mental health facilities, hospitals, and colleges. Check it out if you or someone you love wants to find out more about troubling symptoms.

The Carter Center Mental Health Program (www.cartercenter.org)
If you're interested in joining the fight against the lingering stigma of mental illness, see what the Carter Center is doing to reduce discrimination and improve mental health care availability.

Americans with Disabilities Act (www.usdoj.gov)
Spells out the rights and regulations relating to mental disabilities, and will point you to avenues of assistance if you suspect you are being unfairly or unreasonably treated in work situations.

American Foundation for Suicide Prevention (www.afsp.org)

Children and Adolescents

Bipolar Kids (www.bipolarkids.org)
You'll find here a huge directory of related links to articles about all aspects of bipolar disorder in children and adolescents.

The Bipolar Child (www.bipolarchild.com)
This resource offers current and back newsletters on a variety of subjects related to mood disorders in young people. There's also a useful description of available books.

American Academy of Child and Adolescent Psychiatry (www.aacap.org)
All issues related to children's mental health and well-being, including information about prevention, diagnosis, and treatment. You will find "Facts for Families" about bipolar disorder, depression, ADHD, oppositional defiant disorder, and teen suicide, plus how to locate a child psychiatrist.

Child and Adolescent Bipolar Foundation (www.bpkids.org)
Its stated purpose is to educate, connect, advocate, and support research on pediatric bipolar disorder. You'll find an online newsletter, advice on how to locate a doctor, and a directory of support groups, among much else.

Resources

Psychiatric Organizations

American Psychological Association (www.apa.org)
Go to this site for the American Psychological Association, hit "bipolar disorder," and find a slew of articles about treatment possibilities and variations. You can also request information about certified psychologists in your area.

American Psychiatric Association (www.psych.org)
Go to this site for the American Psychiatric Association, get linked to HealthyMinds, and you will find information on how to locate a certified psychiatrist in your area.

American Association for Marriage and Family Therapy (www.aamft.org)
This resource is designed primarily for practitioners, but you can do a search for a marriage and family therapist in your area.

National Institute of Mental Health (www.nimh.nih.gov)
Offers an extensive list of publications of interest. Much information on research advances, and one of the places you can find a mood chart.

Health and Fitness and Substance Abuse Treatment

Bally Fitness (www.ballyfitness.com)
I use this site to get health information. Most of the information is free. Check it out for suggested diets and workout plans.

Healthmsn.com (www.healthmsn.com)
Articles and news stories related to medications, health, and fitness.

American Dietetic Association (www.eatright.org)
As the site address suggests, this is all about eating right. You will find advice about promoting health and well-being, and where, when, and how to locate a nutritionist.

Substance Abuse and Mental Health Services Administration
(www.samhsa.gov)

SAMHSA is part of the U.S. Department of Health and Human Services. This site is chock-full of all kinds of news, information, and advice. One useful feature will direct you to alcohol abuse treatment programs in your area.

Centers for Disease Control and Prevention (www.cdc.gov)

I use this site to get current statistics about health-related issues. You can also find some great articles.

U.S. Food and Drug Administration (www.fda.gov)

The Food and Drug Administration, also part of the U.S. Department of Health and Human Services, can point you to some useful information about particular medications, drug approvals, and warnings.

National Center for Complementary and Alternative Medicine
(www.nccam.nih.gov)

Check this out for information about dietary and herbal supplements and other non-prescription-medication treatments for depression and other mood disorders. There's also news about current clinical trials.

Food and Nutrition Information Center (www.fnic.nal.usda.gov)

This is an excellent resource for all kinds of solid and practical information on eating in a healthful way. Good for encouragement and advice if fighting weight gain is part of your treatment for bipolar.

SUGGESTED READING

On the Internet you'll find a few thousand titles related to mental illness and bipolar disorder. That's a pile of books! And I haven't read them all! But I've listed here a few that caught my attention and that you may want to look into.

Personal Stories

An Unquiet Mind: A Memoir of Moods and Madness, by Kay Jamison
Jamison, who is both a psychiatrist and a bipolar, writes here what she calls a scientific autobiography—what can be exhilarating and thrilling about the "ups," why it is so tempting to go off the medications, why bipolar people can be so maddening to those around them.

Night Falls Fast: Understanding Suicide, by Kay Jamison
Another inside look at what it's like to suffer from depression. Jamison herself attempted suicide while in her twenties. This can be a painful read sometimes, but it tells a true story, and it's maybe especially useful for those support people who want to know what the endless despair of depression feels like. The book also contributes some well-researched information on the connections between mental illness and suicide, and why more attention needs to be paid.

Darkness Visible: A Memoir of Madness, by William Styron
Styron, now passed away, did not experience bipolar disorder, but suffered from deep, disabling depression. This is a harrowing account of what that descent was like; this, too, is a powerful book because of the marvelous writing.

Suggested Reading

A Brilliant Madness: Living with Manic-Depressive Illness,
by Patty Duke and Gloria Hochman
I have attended conferences with Patty Duke, who's been a spokeswoman in recent years for the National Institute of Mental Health. I know she's a straight-shooting, tell-it-like-it-is kind of individual, and that's what she does in this personal account of her suicide attempts, drug abuse, bad marriages, and her eventual salvation through medication.

Skywriting: A Life Out of the Blue, by Jane Pauley
Pauley, the charming TV personality, wrote this after she was diagnosed and treated for bipolar disorder, which she is convinced ran through her family. Pauley has said, "Bipolar disorder was the first significant illness of my life and it hit me hard," and she spares no details in describing her experiences. She's also now helping to spread the news and fight the stigma by working with the National Mental Health Association.

Practical Advice

New Hope for People with Bipolar Disorder, by Jan Fawcett, M.D.,
Bernard Golden, Ph.D., and Nancy Rosenfeld
These authors are a medical doctor, a psychologist, and a patient, a good combination for producing a well-rounded, all-angles picture of bipolar—a helpful overview about diagnosing, medicating, and treating through psychotherapy and self-help methods. There's especially useful stuff about depression and suicide prevention.

The Bipolar Disorder Survival Guide: What You and Your Family Need to Know, by David J. Miklowitz, Ph.D.
Miklowitz, a professor of psychology, is a leading expert in the research and treatment of bipolar disorder. This book is a broad compilation of information and advice. You'll find a lot of specific ideas here about mood charts, various therapies, family involvement, and much more.

Surviving Manic Depression: A Manual on Bipolar Disorder for Patients, Families, and Providers, by E. Fuller Torrey, M.D.
Torrey is another expert on mental illnesses, the author also of *Surviving Schizophrenia*. This book is a thorough guide to causes and symptoms,

choosing doctors, and adopting a treatment regimen, with extensive news about medications.

Why Am I Up, Why Am I Down? Understanding Bipolar Disorder,
by Roger Granet, M.D., and Elizabeth Ferber
The author, a psychiatrist, offers helpful information on diagnosis and treatment in an easy-to-read question-and-answer format.

Bipolar Disorder: A Guide for Patients and Families,
by Francis Mark Mondimore, M.D.
Mondimore, a psychiatrist, is considered one of the outstanding practitioners in the field of bipolar disorder. Here's a thorough review of symptoms, diagnoses, and medications, including a careful discussion of side effects.

The Bipolar Child: The Definitive and Reassuring Guide to Childhood's Most Misunderstood Disorder, by Demitri Papolos, M.D., and Janice Papolos
The author is one of the leaders in the study and understanding of early-onset bipolar disorder, or in children not yet even adolescents. The book, in its third edition, is an invaluable examination of the most critical issues: the differences in behavior between a bipolar child and a child with ADHD, and why the two are frequently misdiagnosed; why medications used to treat hyperactivity are often all wrong in treating bipolar disorder; the difficulties of medicating children. There's also good information on what these kids most need in the way of supportive family and school environments.

It's Called Work for a Reason!: Your Success Is Your Own Damn Fault,
by Larry Winget
This has nothing to do with bipolar, but it's a great book to kick you in your ass!

ACKNOWLEDGMENTS

There are so many people I would like to thank and acknowledge who have either helped me get where I am at this point or played a major role in my life.

First, those involved in the making of this book. **Lynn Sonberg**: Thanks, Lynn, for taking the time to contact me and offering me this opportunity. Is it okay for me to tell my wife now? (Inside joke.) **Andrea Thompson**: What can I say? You are not only a genius, you are a joy and a blessing. This book would not be if not for you. **Penguin publishing team**: Your determination to bring information to those who need it is honorable and appreciated. Thanks for all your efforts and dedication to your craft, and for giving me the chance to express myself and share my thoughts.

My external support group. **Russell**: You have been my friend for almost my entire life. Thanks for sharing the up, down, sideways, and upside down. And thanks for not running away when you could have easily done so. **Steve**: From driving to school together to driving to speaking events, some of our best times have been in cars (that sounds a tad weird). **Terry**: Your friendship and our relationship are just strange, and I thank God for that. **Ronnie and Mrs. Z.**: Nights by the fire and evenings in hotel rooms eating 'za. Sometimes you never know how much you help someone, but I hope you both know how much you have helped me. **Freddie**: As goofy as you are, it's nice to have you around when a mirror is not handy. Keep dreaming and never allow anyone to take those dreams from you. **Miles**: You have never lied to me, ever. When I sucked you said so; when I could do better you told me; when I was wrong you reminded me; and when I am right, I am sure you will point that out as well. **Kevin**: "Nobody Knows but Me" may be a hit song to your fans, but to me it is a story of my life. Your voice has changed the lives of so many. I am blessed to be one of them. I hope someday you'll pick up the phone and call. **Ann**: Speaking to your nurses has not only provided me with insight into your field, but allowed me to be a part of their new journey. Thanks for your support. **Mr. Dever**: Your kindness to me and my family will always be appreciated and never forgotten. You are a good man with a huge heart. **Mr. LeMay**: I have told you often and I will say it again here and now: I truly love you. Jim, you saved my life. My wife, children, and I can never begin to thank you enough. While I must say that sometimes your way of looking through me is a little unnerving, your way of looking at me has given me my confidence back.

My internal support group. **Mom (BJ)**: If not for the way you raised us to be tough, responsible people, I would have never been able to catch the hole in the wall and hang on. I love you very much and respect everything you have done. **Dad**: I wish you were here in body. Your strength, courage, and commitment are the reasons I was able to climb back up the wall. **My brothers and sister**: I hope someday we can sit in a room together again and I really hope that one of us is not in a box when that happens. Life is terribly short. **Bobby and M.**: Thank you for not throwing me out of the family and for allowing me to marry your daughter. **The Muenchen clan**: I am sure I owe someone some money somehow. Through everything, you could have very well turned your back on me, and yet you never did. The word "in-laws" does not apply to you; you are family through and through.

My lifeline. **Dr. Steve**: You're kind, compassionate, caring, and most of all, understanding. I wish every doctor was like you, because I think then we would see many fewer people afraid to ask for help. **My children**: It would take a book of its own to write what I truly should write to you. You have seen, heard, and lived through everything. Your mother and I have been open and honest with you for a reason, and you know what those reasons are. Your hearts are as big as the day is long, your minds are as open as the sky is wide, and because of that, if you stay the course and step up to the plate when you should you will be just fine. I love you guys so much. I want to thank you for not giving up on your old dad. I want to thank you for allowing me to be who I am and for not being (as) mortified as you probably could be. I want to thank you for believing in your mother and me, and trusting that what we say is at the very least in your best interest. I want to thank you for not making me go bipolar as much as you could. Thanks, guys! **Lisa:** I would have to write three books to say what I have to say to you. From the day I saw you walk into the bar, I knew I would be with you for the rest of my life. You should have run like hell instead of into it. You are my best friend, my wife, my life. Your trust in me has not only helped me get to the places I have been, but it is the reason I am willing to fail in order to win. I want to thank you for doing such a great job of holding our family together during the years I was trying to blow it up. I am so proud of you for everything you have done. You are the true celebrity in our house. Thanks for not throwing me away. I love you.

God. Even though I could not understand it while it was happening, I want to thank you for putting me through everything and for putting me in the positions you chose to place me. I do not pretend to understand, but I can honestly say that I am honored that you have provided me with all the good, the bad, and the ugly. It has allowed me to see that in order to get to the good, sometimes you have to go through some really bad, ugly stuff. Thank you, **God**!